Mel Bay Presents

Shady Grove

Mandolin Solos by

David Grisman

with Melodies and Chords

transcribed by John McGann

CD CONTENTS*

1. Shady Grove [4:19]
2. Stealin' [3:31]
3. Off to Sea Once More [5:48]
4. The Sweet Sunny South [3:25]
5. Louis Collins [5:57]
6. Fair Ellender [6:05]
7. Jackaroo [4:02]
8. Casey Jones [4:07]
9. Dreadful Wind and Rain [4:46]
10. I Truly Understand [3:40]
11. The Handsome Cabin Boy [6:13]
12. Whiskey in the Jar [4:14]
13. Down in the Valley [4:59]

*This book is available as a book only or as a book/compact disc configuration.

A compact disc (98718CD) of the music in this book is now available. The publisher strongly recommends the use of these recordings along with the text to insure accuracy of interpretation and ease in learning.

The CD is produced by Acoustic Disc Records.
Pages 93-96 were left blank intentionally.

1 2 3 4 5 6 7 8 9 0

© 2002 BY MEL BAY PUBLICATIONS, INC., PACIFIC, MO 63069.
ALL RIGHTS RESERVED. INTERNATIONAL COPYRIGHT SECURED. B.M.I. MADE AND PRINTED IN U.S.A.
No part of this publication may be reproduced in whole or in part, or stored in a retrieval system, or transmitted in any form or by any means, electronic, mechanical, photocopy, recording, or otherwise, without written permission of the publisher.

Visit us on the Web at www.melbay.com — E-mail us at email@melbay.com

Contents

Shady Grove • 4

Stealin' • 9

Off to Sea Once More • 15

Louis Collins • 22

Fair Ellender • 32

Jackaroo • 45

Casey Jones • 50

Dreadful Wind and Rain • 58

The Handsome Cabin Boy • 61

Whiskey in the Jar • 71

Down in the Valley • 82

Introduction

As a longtime fan of David Grisman's music, I am honored to have transcribed the music contained in this book. The *Shady Grove* album contains some wonderful performances by both David and Jerry Garcia, two of American music's greatest players. This book will provide insight into the art of accompaniment mandolin playing as well as soloing. I have included some performance notes to help you get the most from the transcriptions. Of course, be sure to listen closely to the CD (MB98718) to get all the nuances of touch and tone that defy notation.

Shady Grove
(mandola)

The mandola is the deep voiced counterpart of the viola, tuned CGDA, a fifth below the tuning of the mandolin. As you'll notice, the GDA strings correspond exactly to the bottom three strings of the mandolin, so as a mandolinist, "finding your way" on the mandola isn't too hard; it's a matter of either convincing yourself that everything you knew as G is now C, or "think in a different key"- if you play this mandola solo on the mandolin as written in tab, you'll be playing in A minor rather than D minor. Some players find it easiest to deal with the tuning as a "new instrument", others will think in a transposed key in relation to the fingering ("The band is in D, so if I think A..."). I have chosen to notate this solo in treble clef, as read by mandolinist, rather than the alto (viola) clef, which is a real mandolist's specialty.

Most of the single line playing is in the mandolin register, but the size of the instrument and thicker string gauges give the notes more heft. You'll also get up the neck a bit...and check out the power of the lower chord voicings!

The intro/outro section states the melody, and the subsequent two solos extend the basic melodic material. Look for the bluesy turns of phrase in bars 32-33.

Bar 36 begins a passage which alternates fingered notes with the open D string.

At bar 40, play the 3rd fret C note with your first finger, 5th fret D with the 2nd finger, and 8th fret F with the 4th finger. The open A string before and after this phrase allow you to smoothly shift position.

Shady Grove

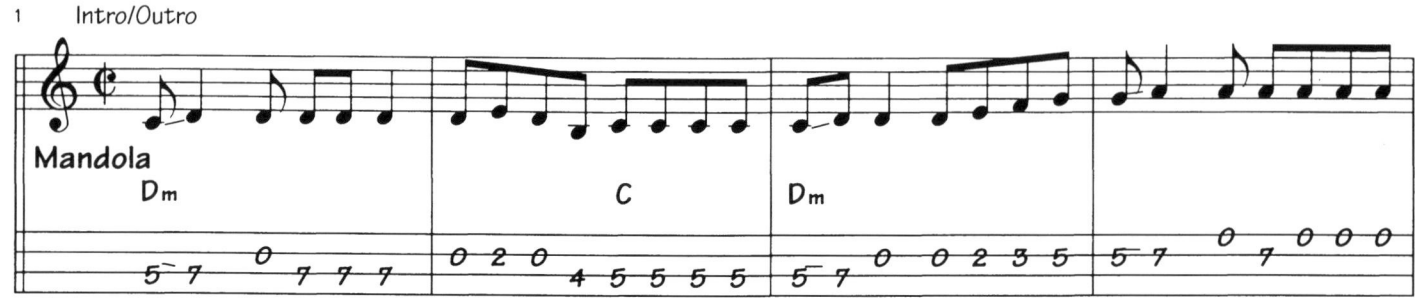

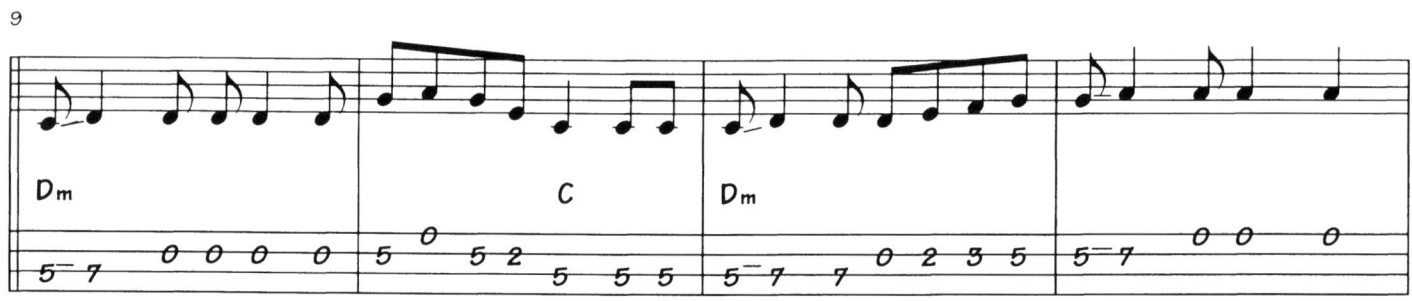
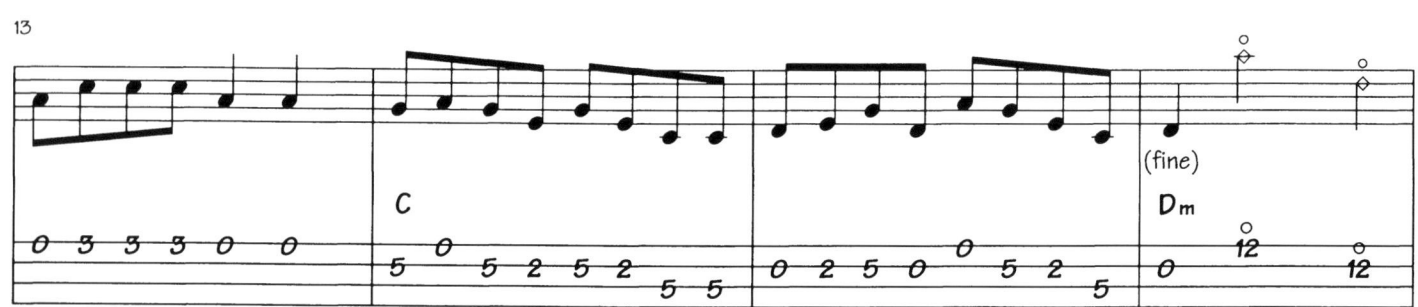

© DAWG Music. All rights reserved. Used by permission.

17

20 verses/choruses/guitar solos
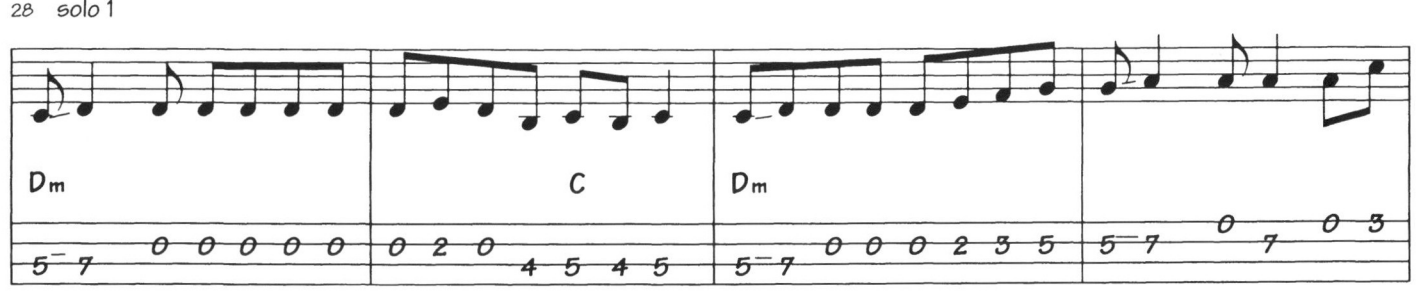

28 solo 1
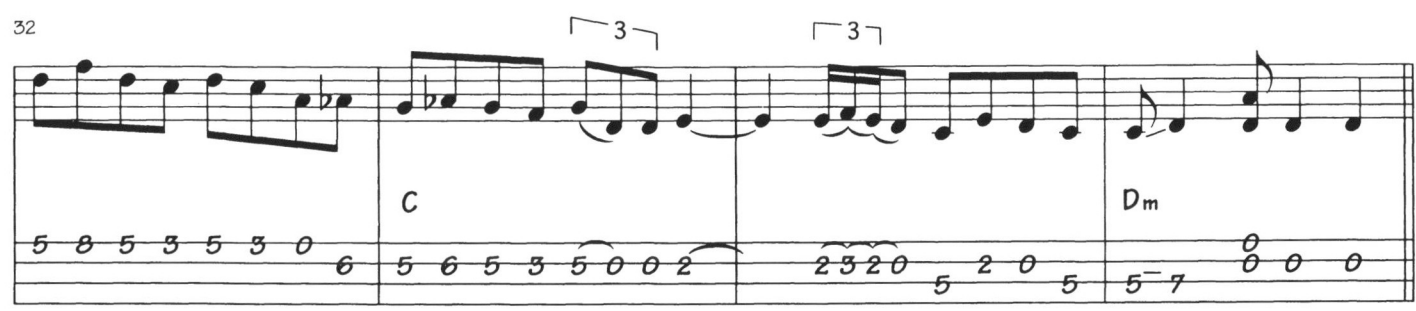

32

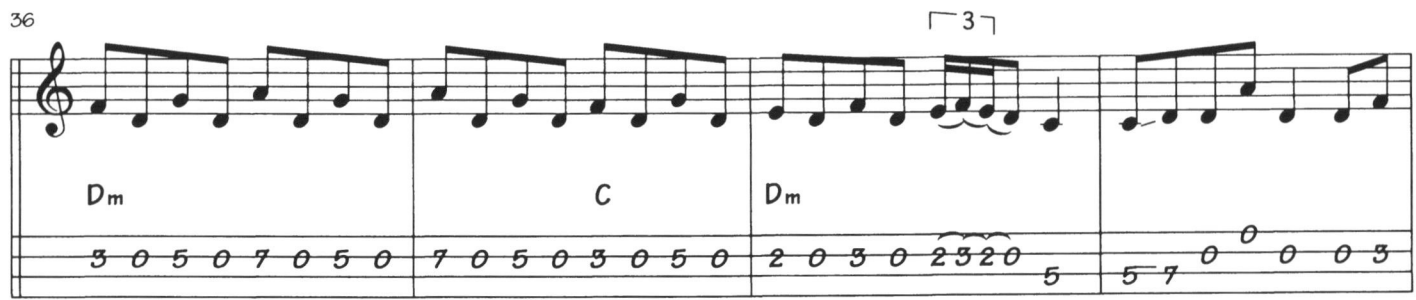
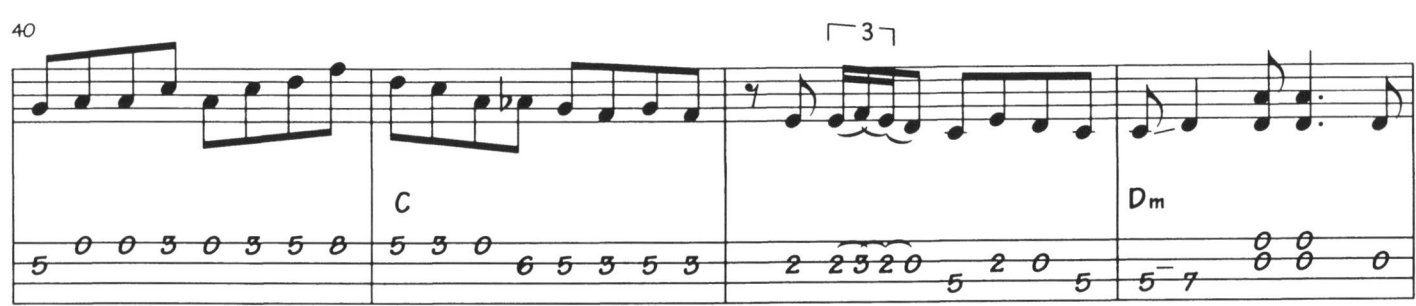
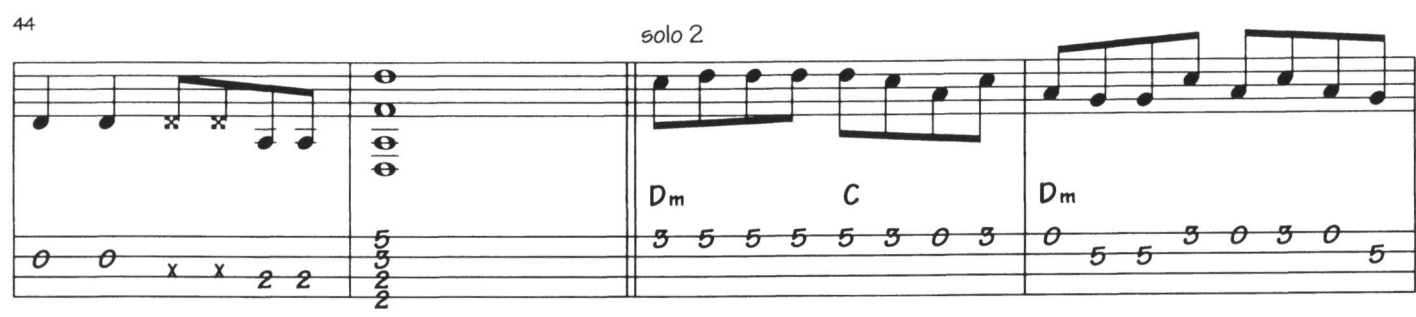
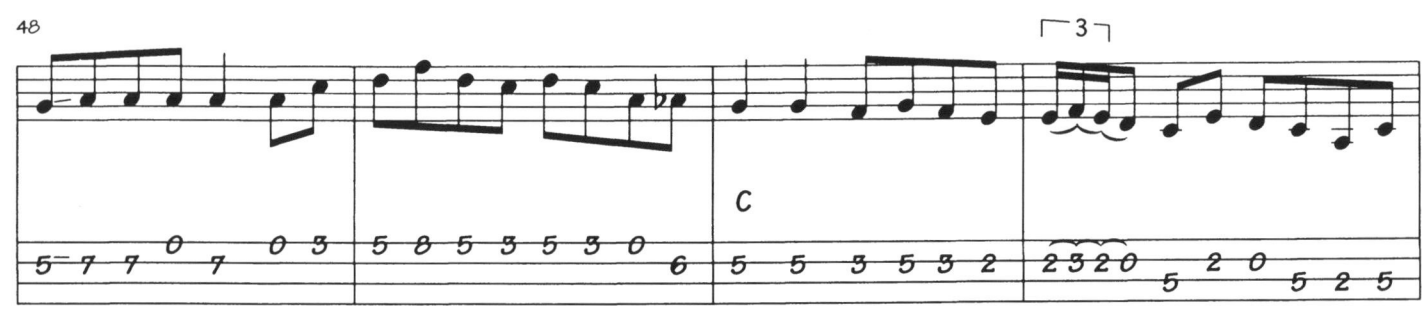

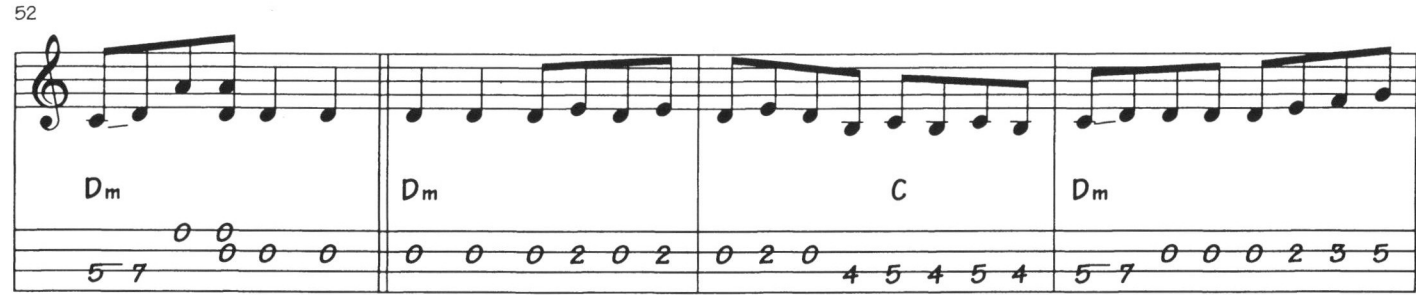

*This page has been
left blank to avoid
awkward page turns*

Stealin'

What could be funkier than the sound of the banjolin, the mandolin-banjo? You can play all this music on the standard mandolin, but for the ultimate in stacatto attack (non-sustaining notes), or *spank*, dust off your banjolin and dig in with downstrokes on all but the tremolo notes. It is a good exercise in articulation to play the various passages first with alternating down/up/down/up picking, then with all downstrokes, and note the contrast in attack and emphasis between the two picking styles.

The intro begins with chords under the guitar for 4 bars, then the manjo rises to the top with some melody. The bluesy phrase at bar 16 is a hook which recurs throughout the piece.

The solo at bar 50 starts with some nice phrases that uses chromatic E♭s and B♭s.

Bar 52 can be fingered out of third position (the first finger taking the third fret, 2nd finger at the 5th fret, 4th finger at the 8th fret) with the open 1st string in bar 53 allowing a return to first position.

Bar 58's repeated G notes (remember to use all downstrokes) are reminiscent of Bill Monroe and Earl Scruggs.

There is such a great "jug band feel" to this track!

Stealin'

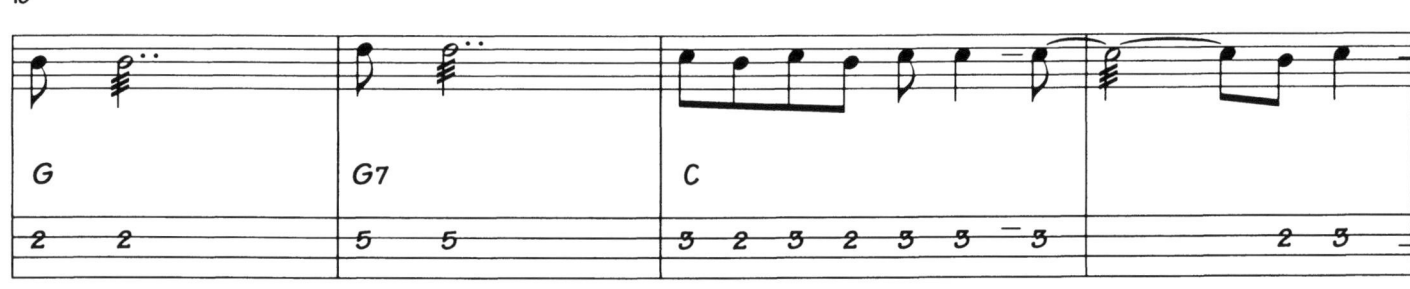

© DAWG Music. All rights reserved. Used by permission.

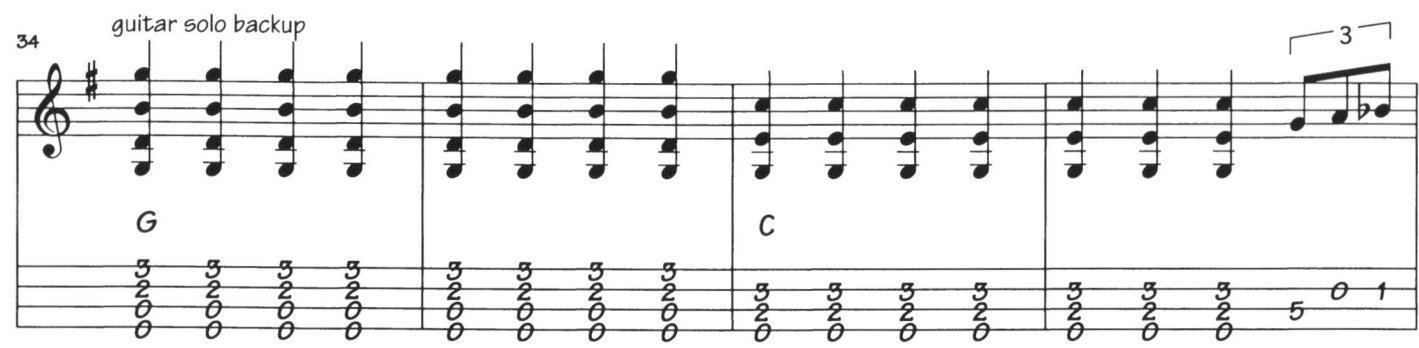

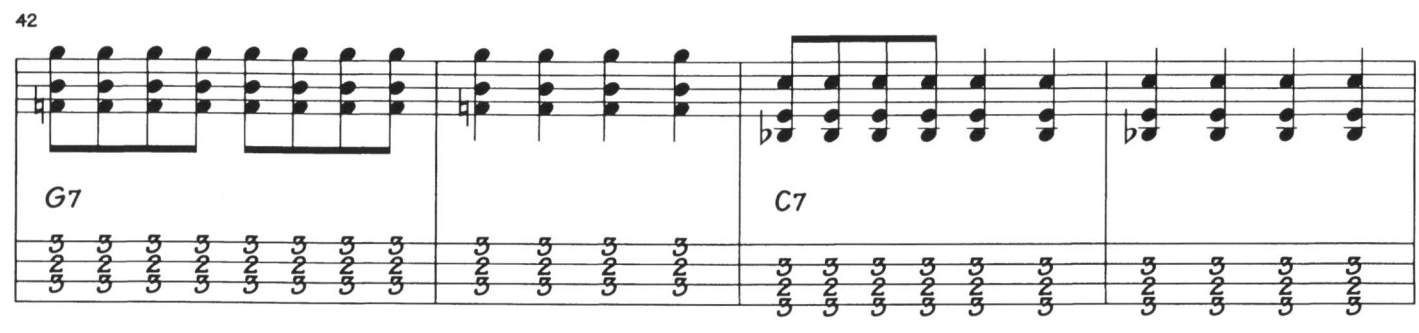
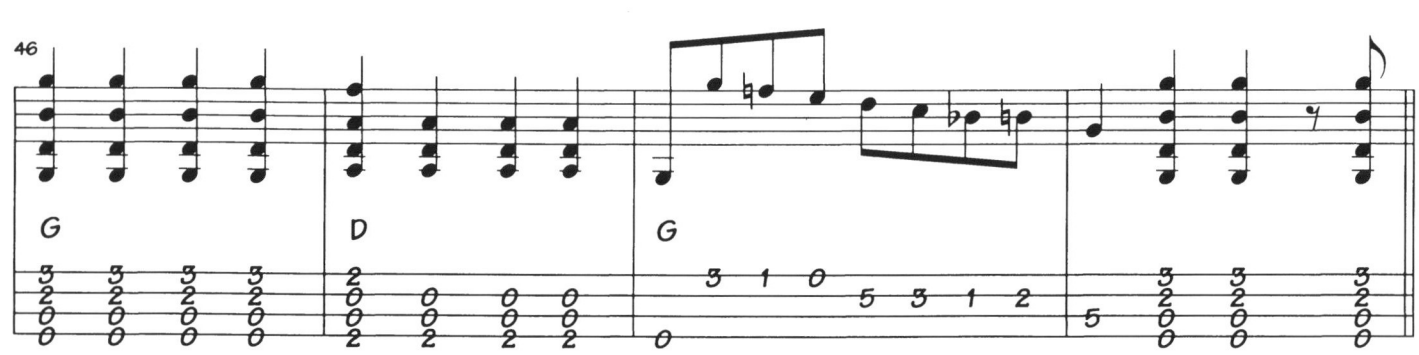

*This page has been
left blank to avoid
awkward page turns*

Off to Sea Once More

This track is a primer for mandolinists to learn to vary the melody of a traditional tune in interesting ways that never stray too far from the original thread of the tune.

The intro is played rubato (in free time without a pulse). Bar 6 begins time, into the first melody statement, which is derived from the first 8 bars of the vocal melody.

Solo 1 revisits the melody at bar 6 an octave higher.

Solo 2 extends the previous melody across the entire song form, in the lower register. Look for the subtle variations in note and rhythm choices.

Solo 3 is similar to the intro and solo 1's 8 bar form, this time played in the higher octave.

Solo 4 is the same form as solo 2, but now in the higher octave. Listen to the distinctive tone of the notes voiced high on the 2nd string, measures 124-130. The same notes played on the first string have a very different sound and effect.

Solo 5 repeats the intro form and register.

Solo 6 is quite similar to solo 5, this time in the higher octave and ending with harmonics.

Off to Sea Once More

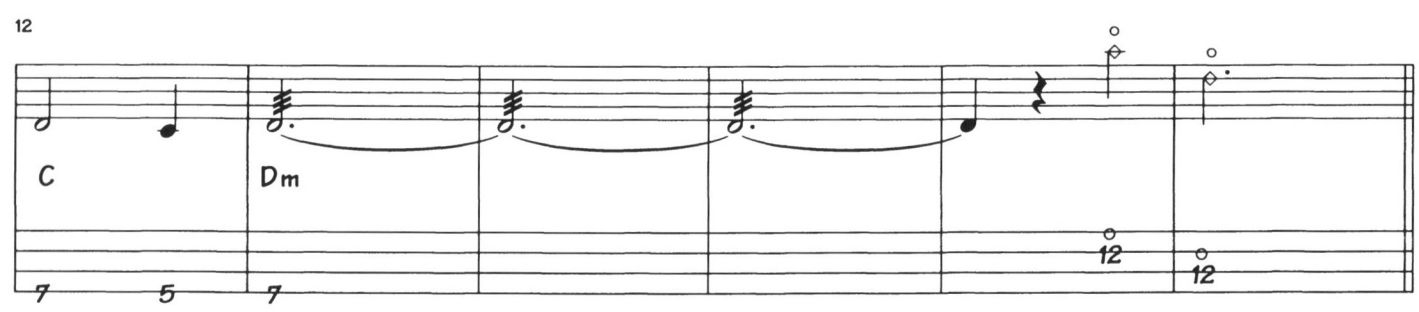

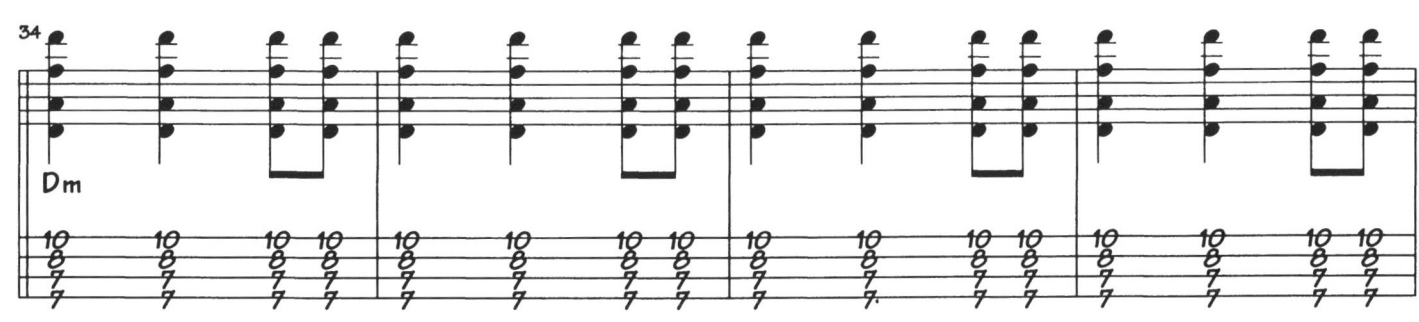

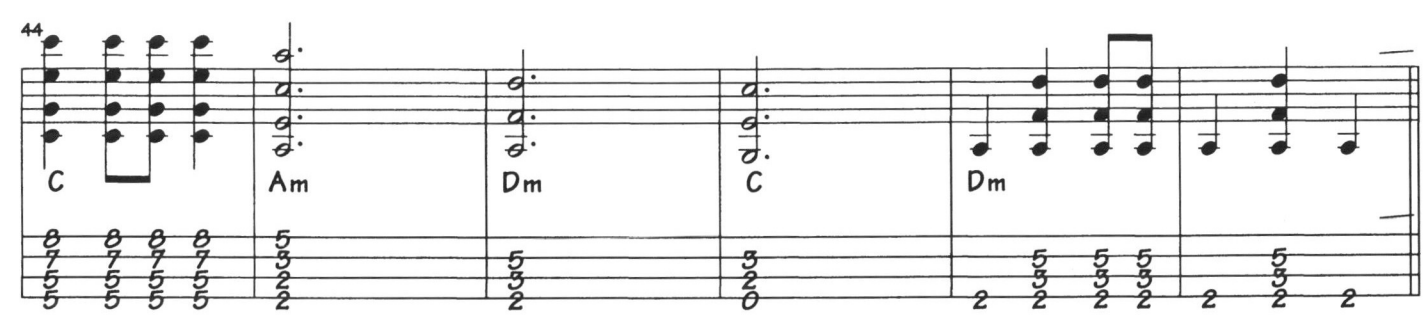

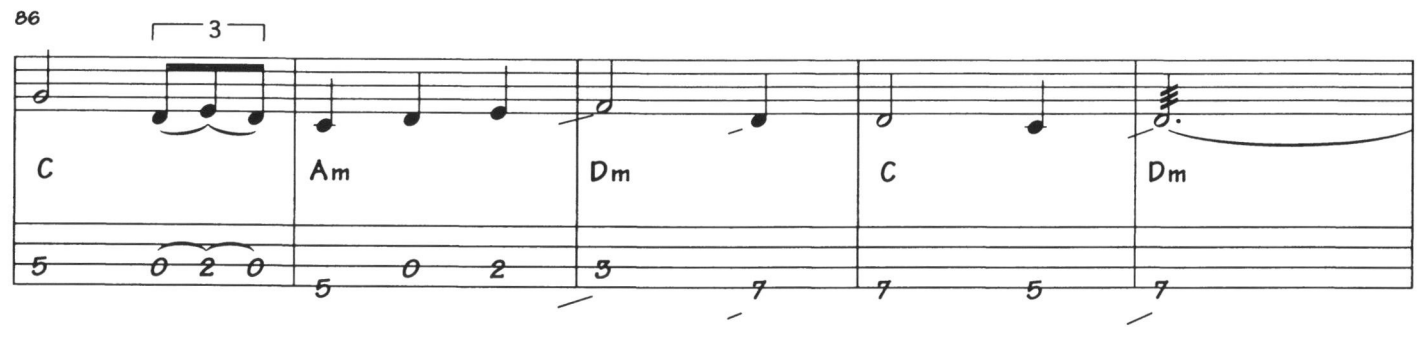
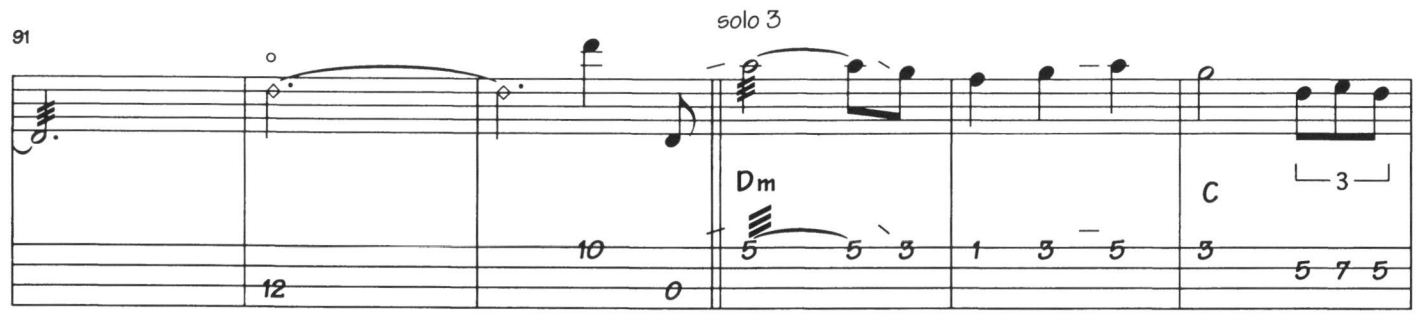

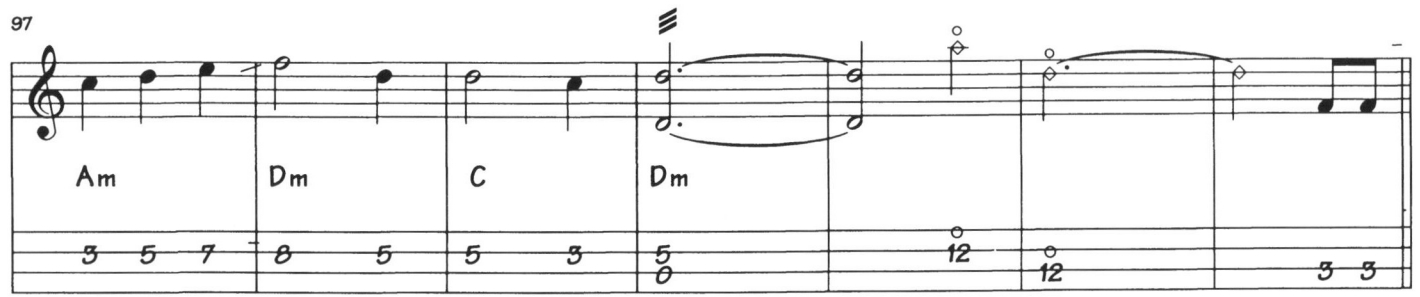
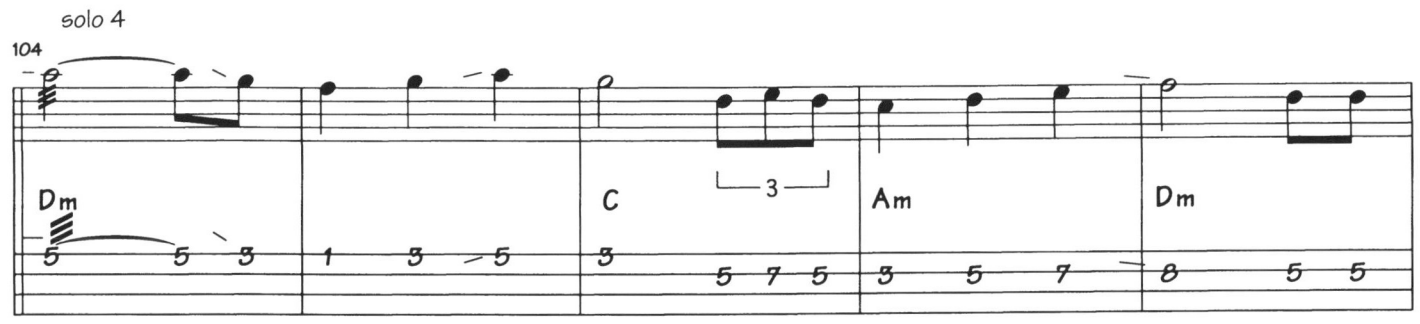

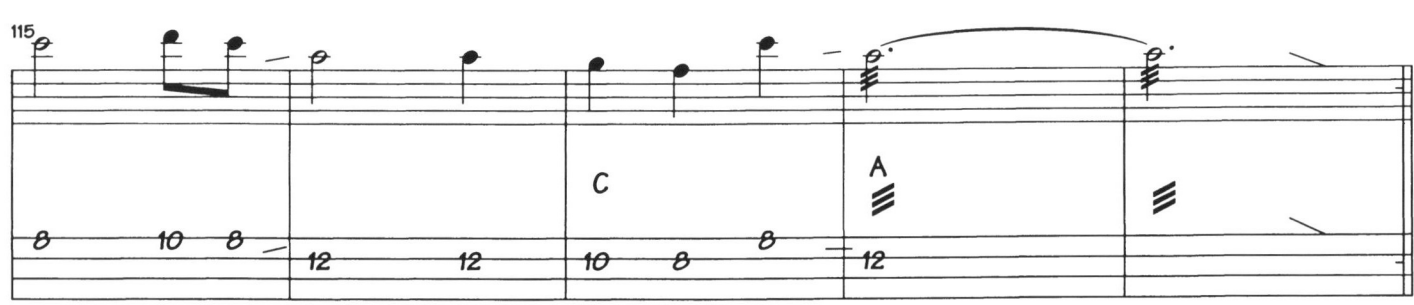

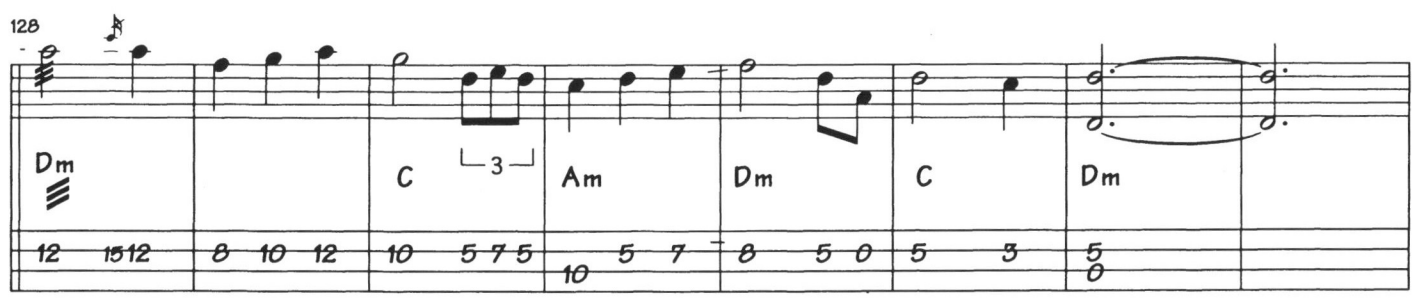
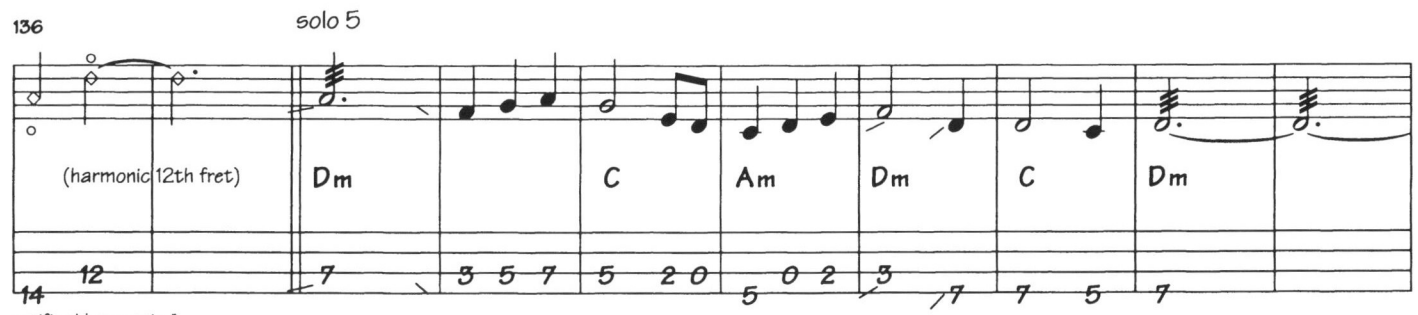

artifical harmonic *
* (finger A 2nd fret, sound harmonic at 14th w/right index finger)

artifical harmonic *
* (finger E 2nd fret, sound harmonic at 14th w/right index finger)

Louis Collins

Listen for the interaction between Jerry's guitar and David's mandolin-interactive listening is the key to co-creating music that sounds alive.

The solos never stray very far from the melodic structure of the song. Compare the various solos here for the subtle differences in phrasing and note choices.

Tremolo sets the mood on the entrance at bar 8, which shifts into some nicely textured rhythm playing at bar 14. At the third bar of the chorus (bar 40), there is a very effective melodic fill between the vocal lines.

Verse 2 backup combines chordal textures with some single note phrases.

Chorus 2 adds some tremolo to the texture.

Solo 2 starts with tremolo, and at 88 expands the phrase used in solo 1, bar 54. As the phrase happens a little sooner in the soloing form, it feels like a development of the original idea. This is an organic expansion of a melodic idea, which is very different from the "hot licks" mentality of "insert lick here".

Chorus 3 and Guitar solo 3 backup present some arpeggiated backup, meaning that the chord tones are played one at a time in a rolling, melodic fashion.

Solo 3 has some nice syncopation, again revisits the melodic idea from bar 54, and launches into some beautifully smooth tremolo.

Solo 4 again restates the melody with variations in phrasing.

The ending solo develops the idea in bar 54 to a high point with the high C note in bar 196. Again, it is worth mentioning the idea-and-development aesthetic that gives improvisation a storytelling-like quality.

Louis Collins

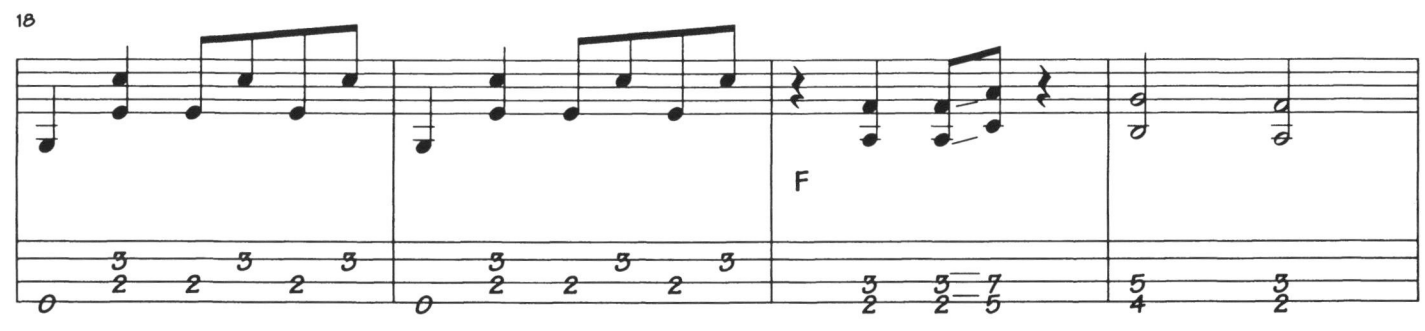

© 1963, Renewed 1991 by Winwood Music Co., Inc. All rights reserved. Used by permission.

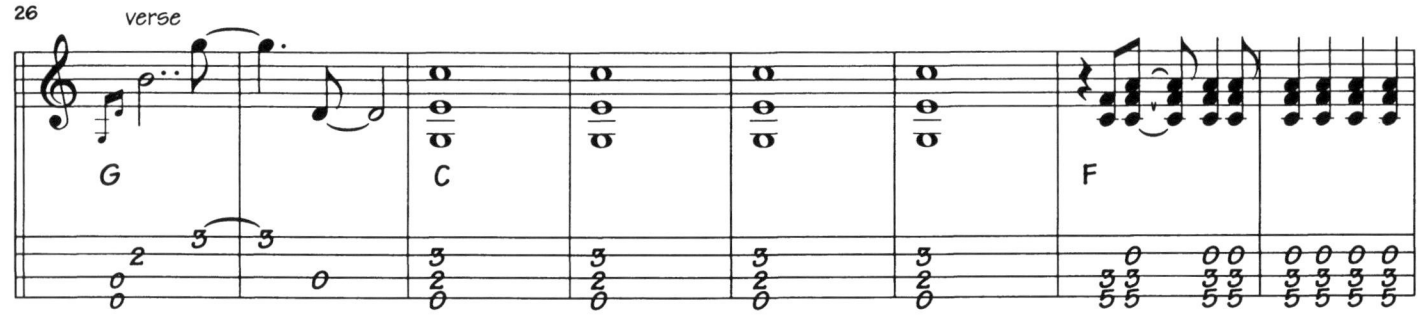
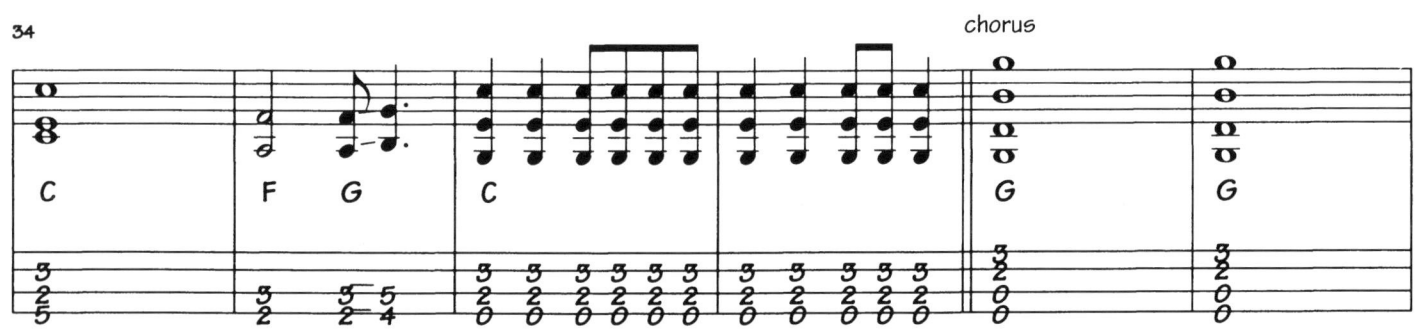

24

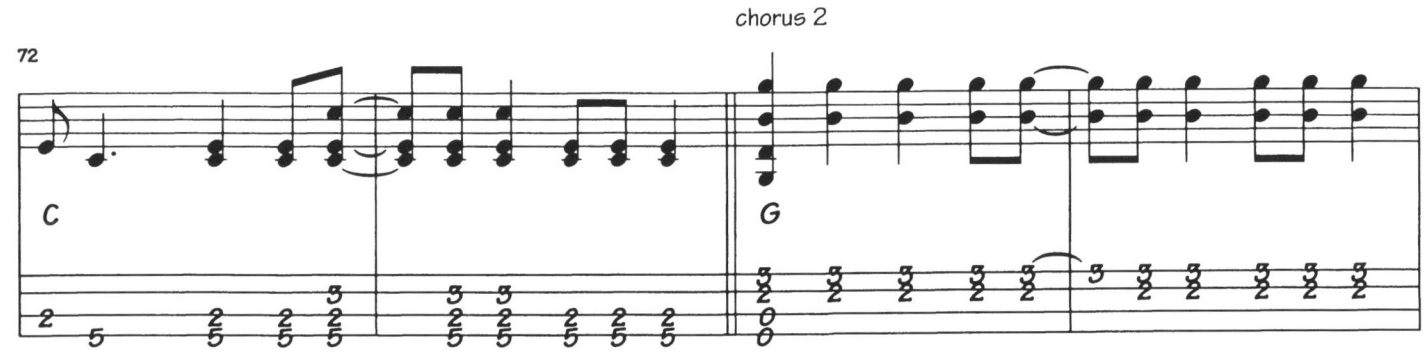

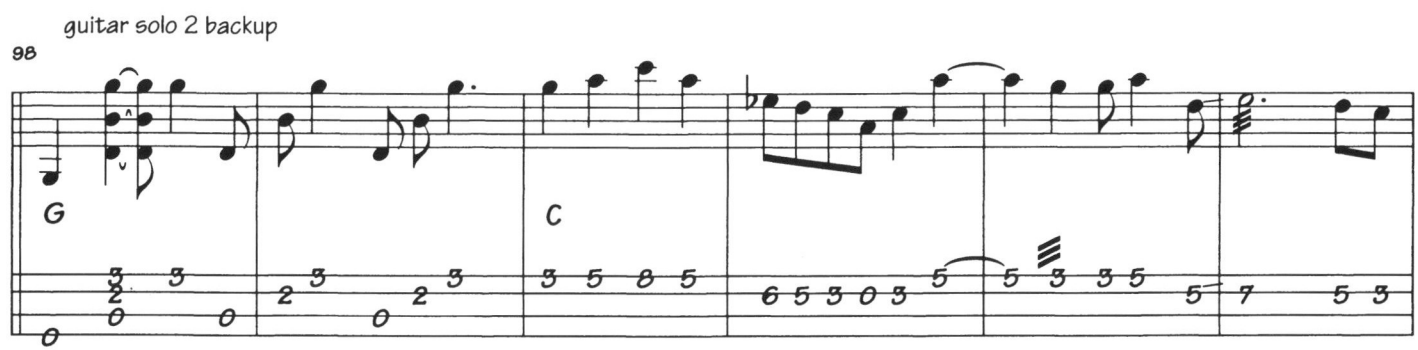

28

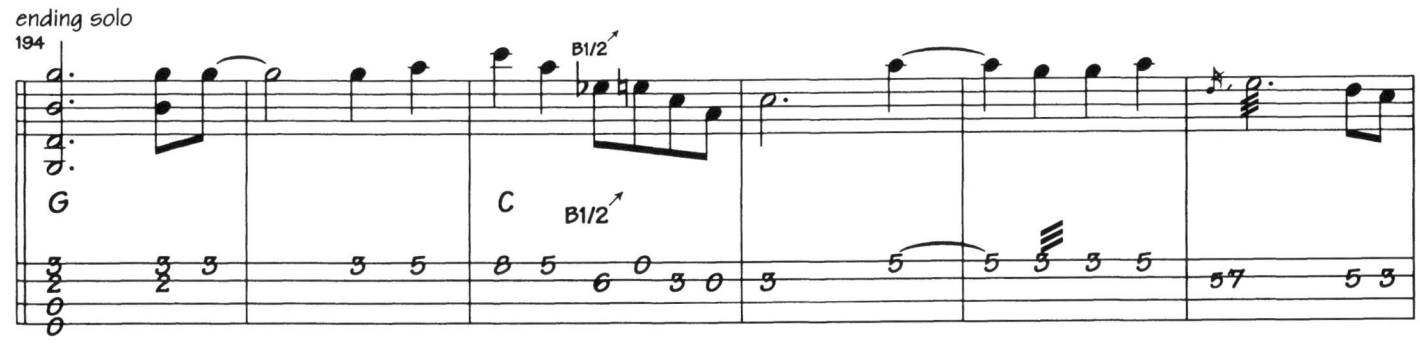

Fair Ellender

High register tremolo introduces this ballad, again drawing directly from the vocal melody of the song. Notice the effective use of space in the backup to the first verse, where entire bars go by without mandolin.

Tremolo is used throughout this tune, and sounds to me to be based on a 16th note attack (four strokes per downbeat). Keep a relaxed wrist!

The note choices vary, sometimes harmonizing the melody, at 190 harmonizing with the flute solo, and at other times creating counter melodies based on the chords.

Fair Ellender

Traditional
Arr. by Jerry Garcia
& David Grisman
Adapted from Mike Seeger

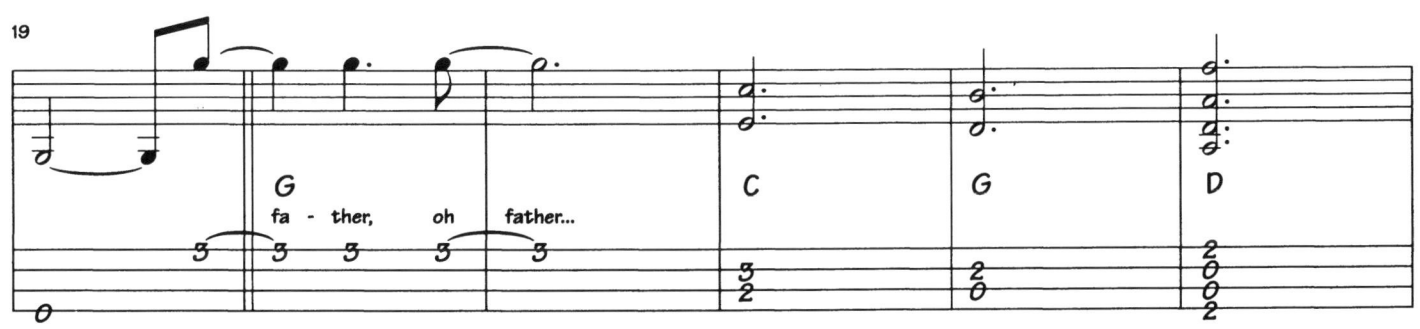

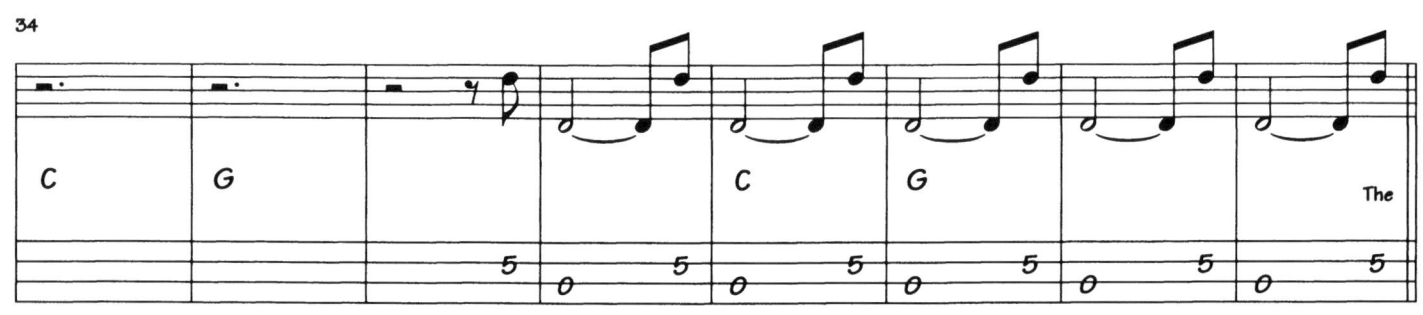
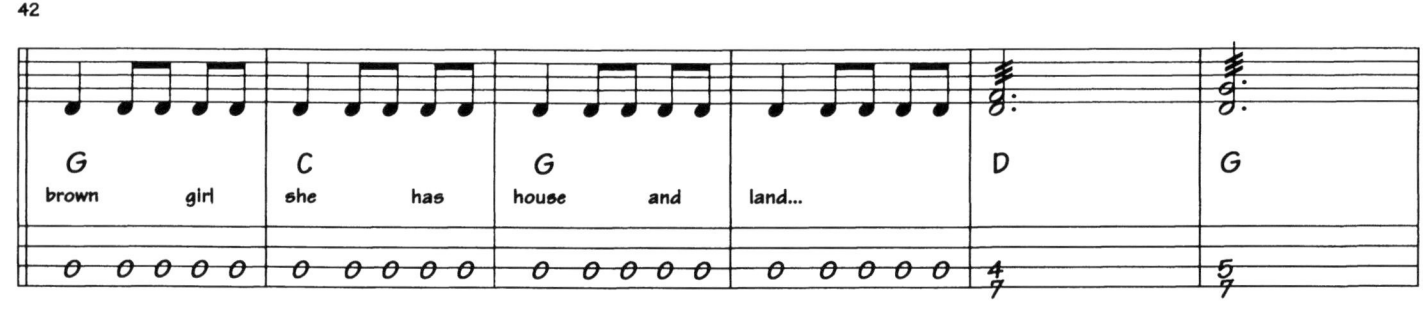
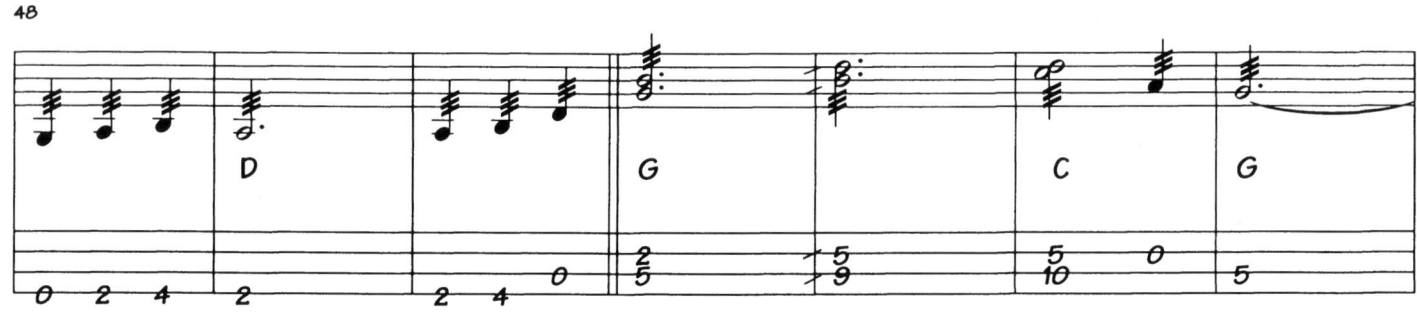

34

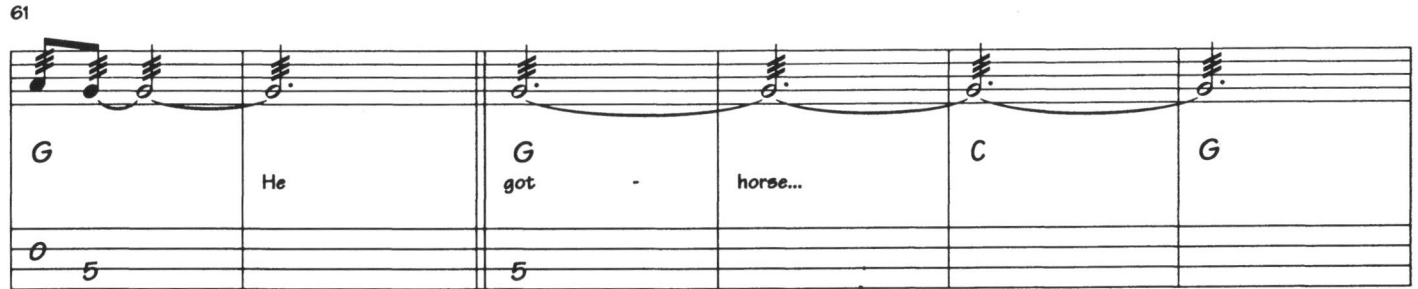
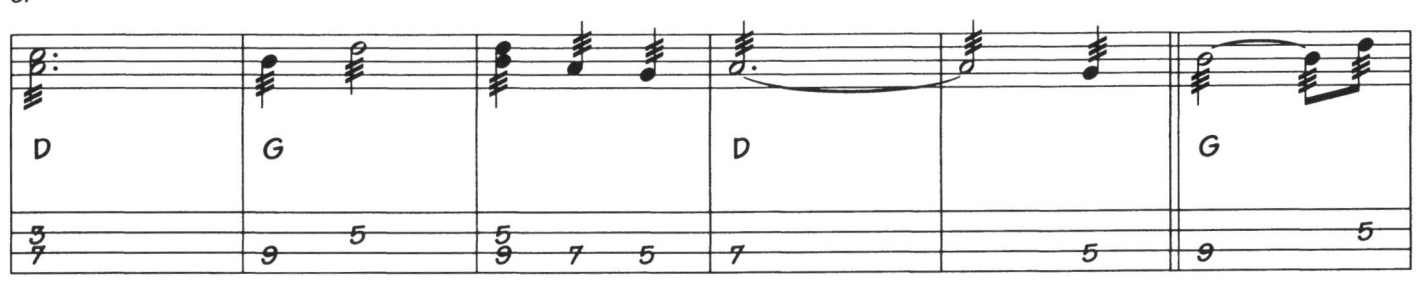

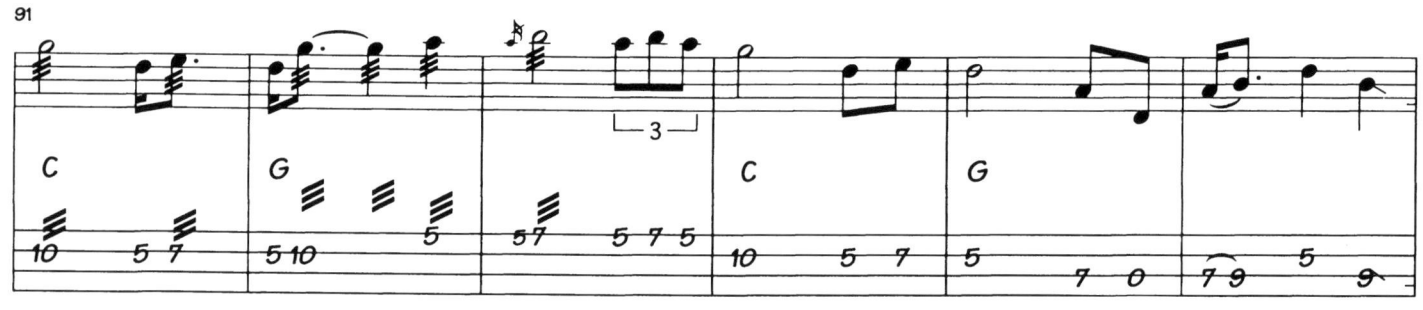
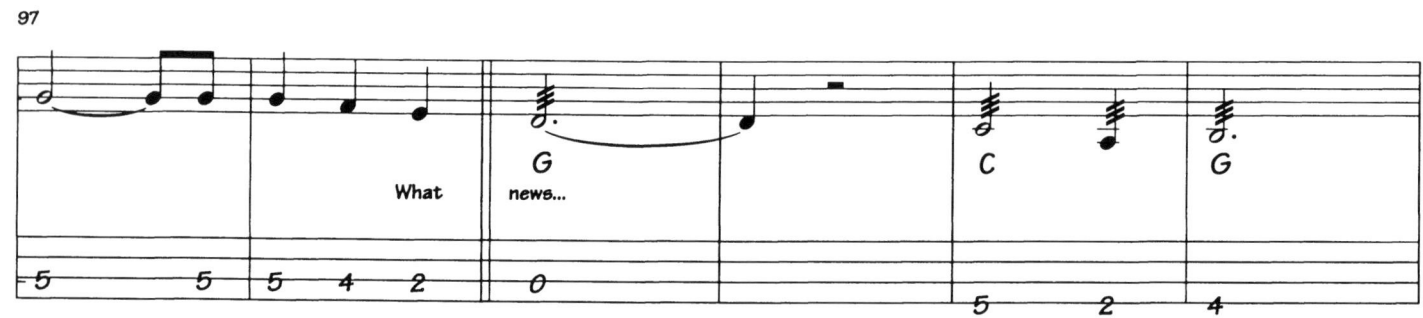

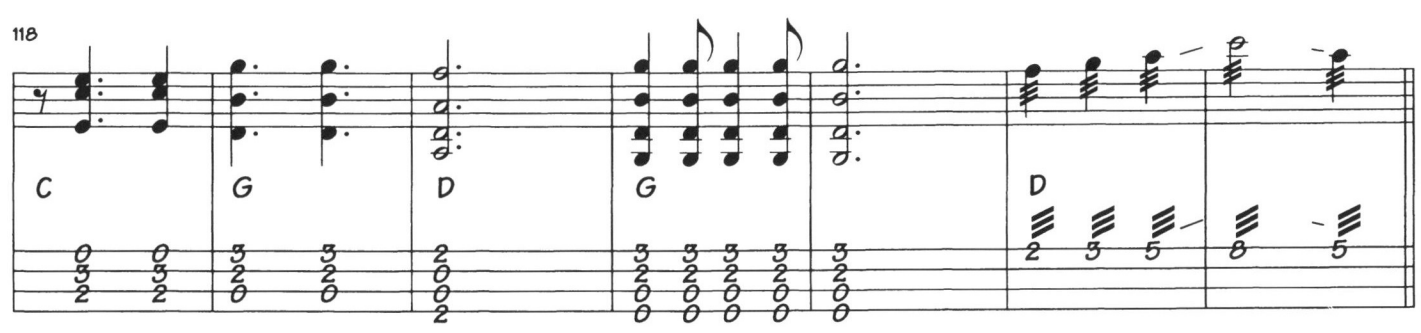

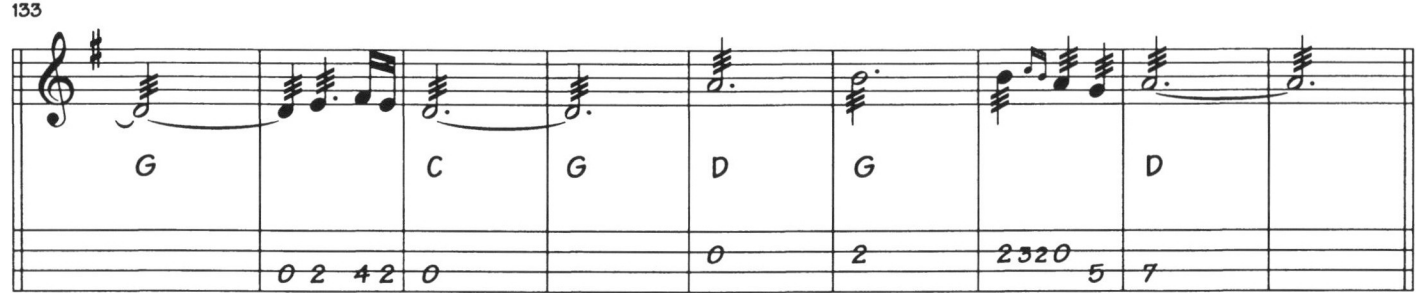

She turned...

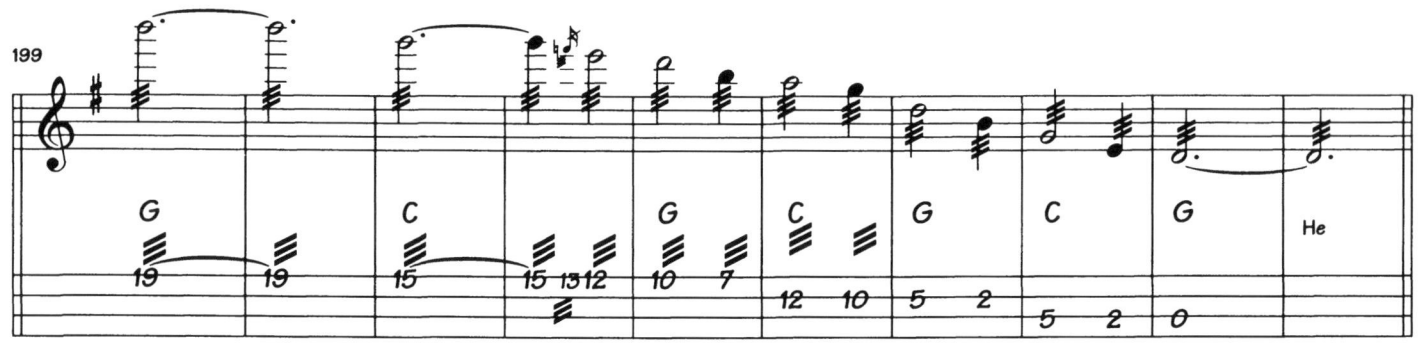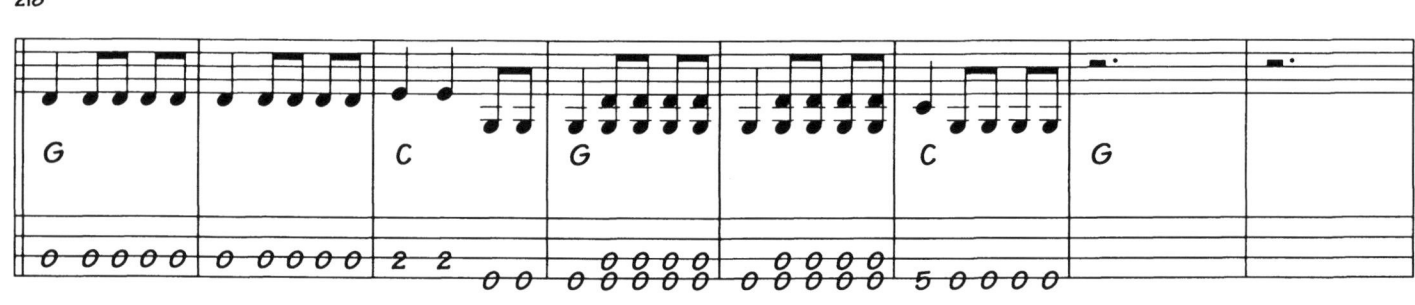

41

43

*This page has been
left blank to avoid
awkward page turns*

Jackaroo

An uptempo Em romp, with some very Grismanesque mandolin.

The mando solo at bar 24 features some classic Dawg phraseology, from the pentatonic lead in notes through the zigzag lines in bars 24-25 and the patterns in bars 30-31.

The Gmaj7 sound in bar 32 is unexpected and delicious! The solo continues with some chordal passages, double stops and tremolo.

Bar 45 begins with a nice unison phrase on the fingered and open E notes, working down the scale to the triplet double pull-off in bar 49, and ending with some syncopation in bar 51 and the bluesy hook line at bars 52-54.

Jackaroo

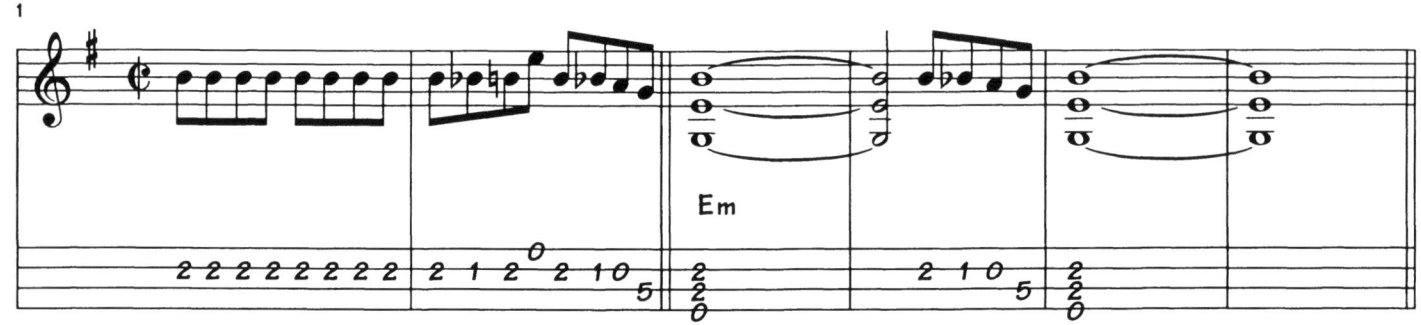

progression for verses and guitar solo

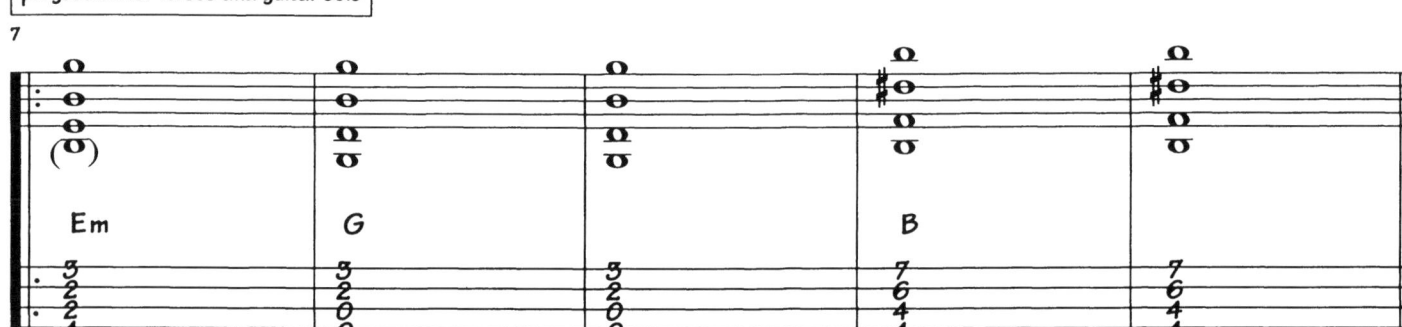

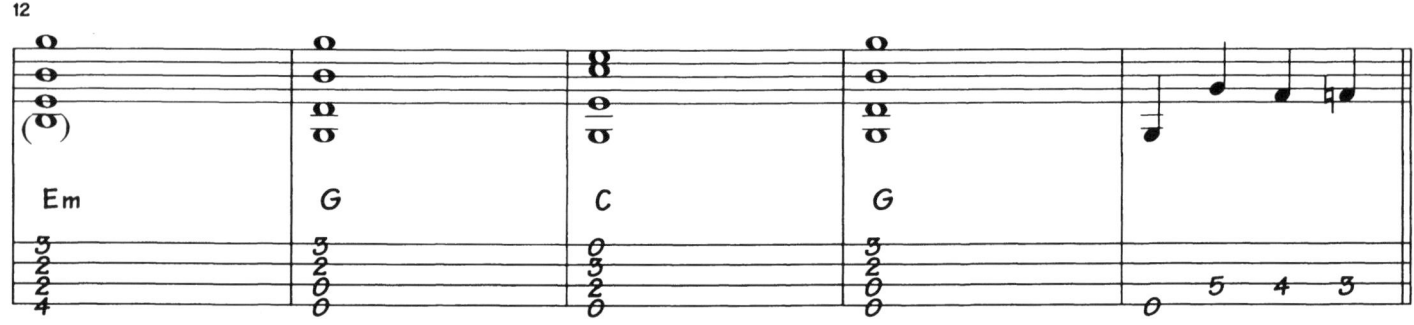

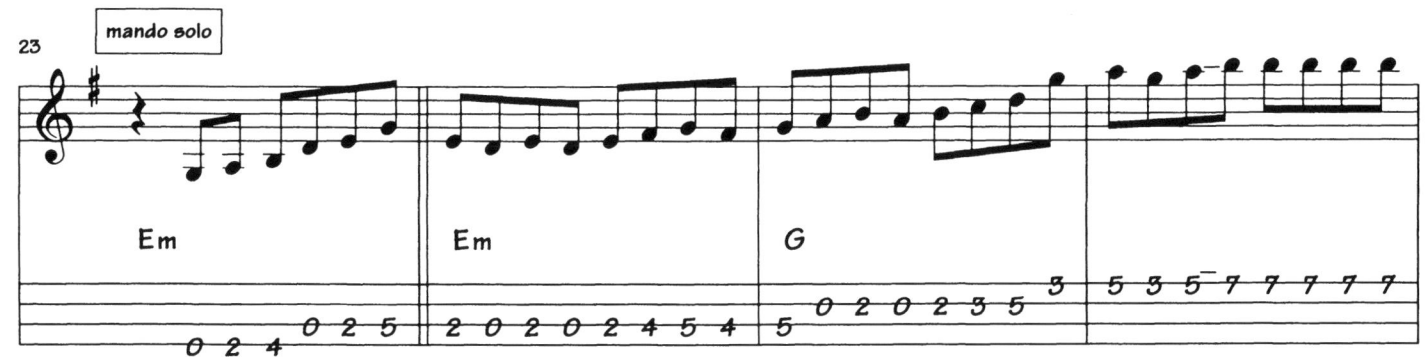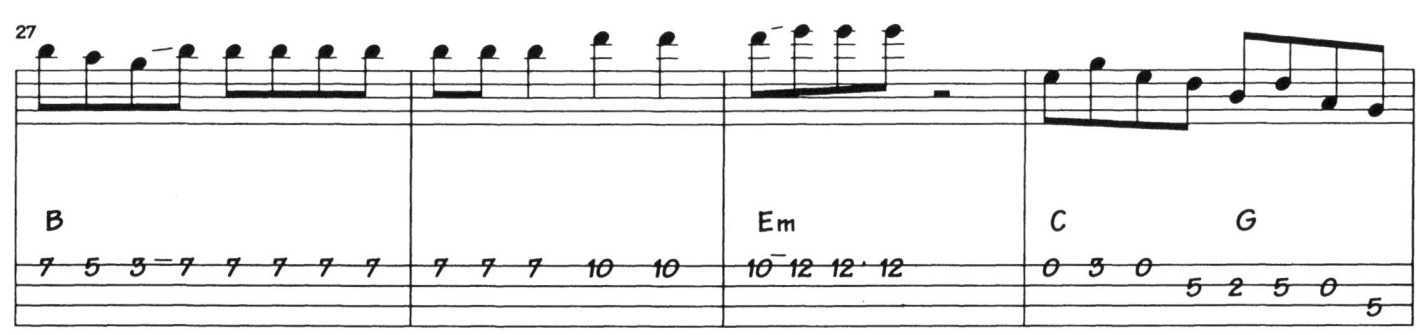

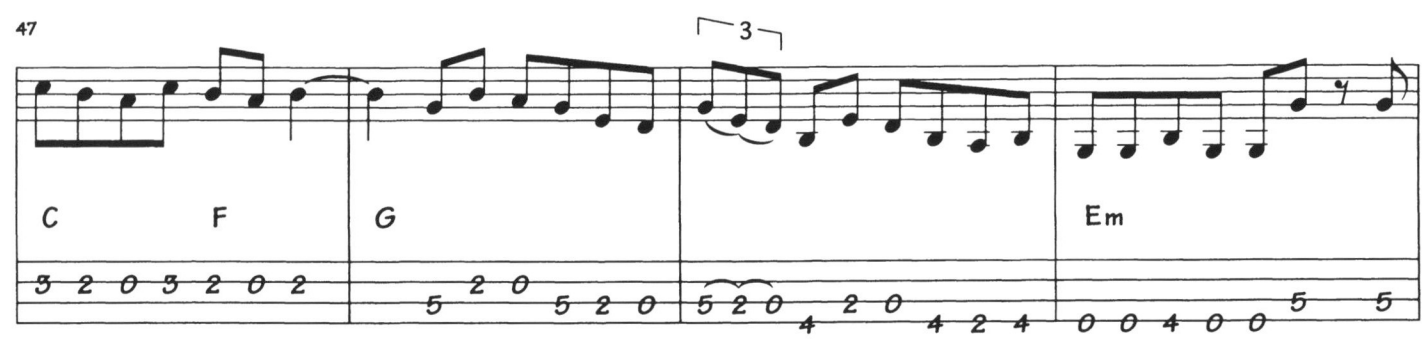

48

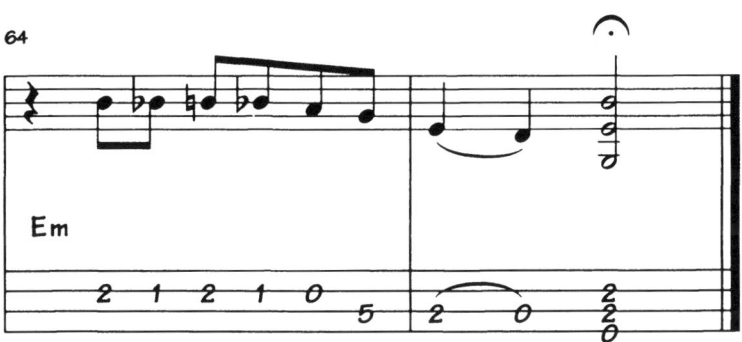

Casey Jones

The intro mandolin plays melody with the guitar, setting up a mood that carries through the song.

Verse 1 starts with some tremolo backup, and develops into some melody doubling with the voice and guitar.

Solo 1 varies the approach of the intro slightly.

Verse 2 follows the approach of verse one. Listen to the interplay in the last 2 bars (70-71) where Jerry plays a melodic phrase that is echoed with slightly different note choices in bar 71.

Verse 3 backup sticks close to Jerry's vocal.

Solo 2 is played working with the lines in the guitar solo, but an octave higher.

Verse 4 uses some muted notes that give an almost Reggae style rhythmic feel to the backup.

Verse 5 returns to the previous appraoch of doubling the melody.

The last solo follows the melody with a few melodic interjections at 144 and 146.

Casey Jones

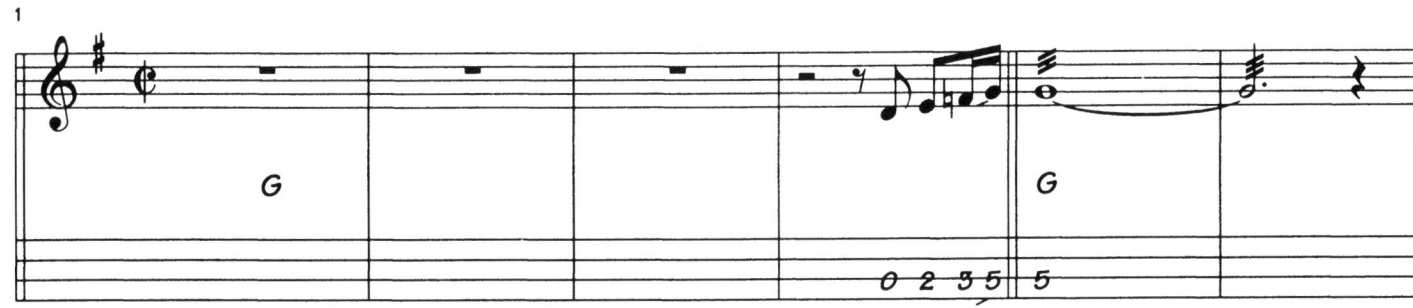

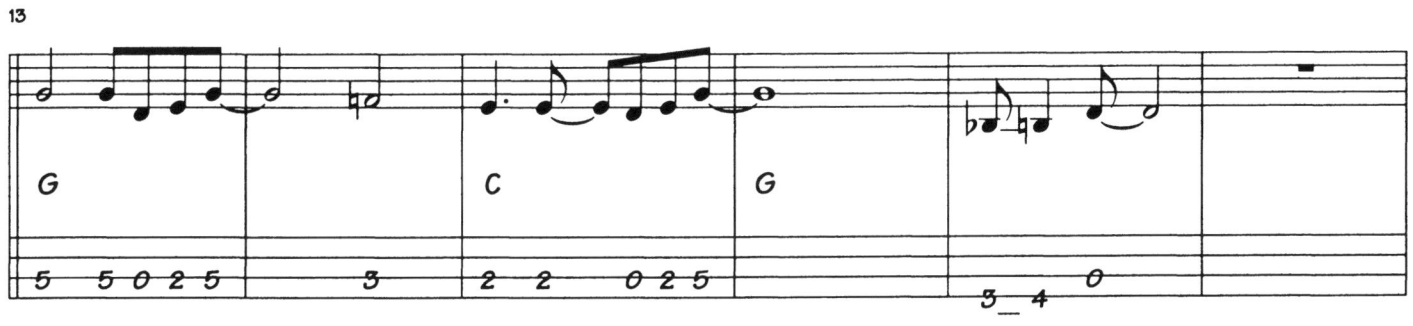

verse 1

© 1976 by Wynwood Music Co., Inc. All rights reserved. Used by permission.

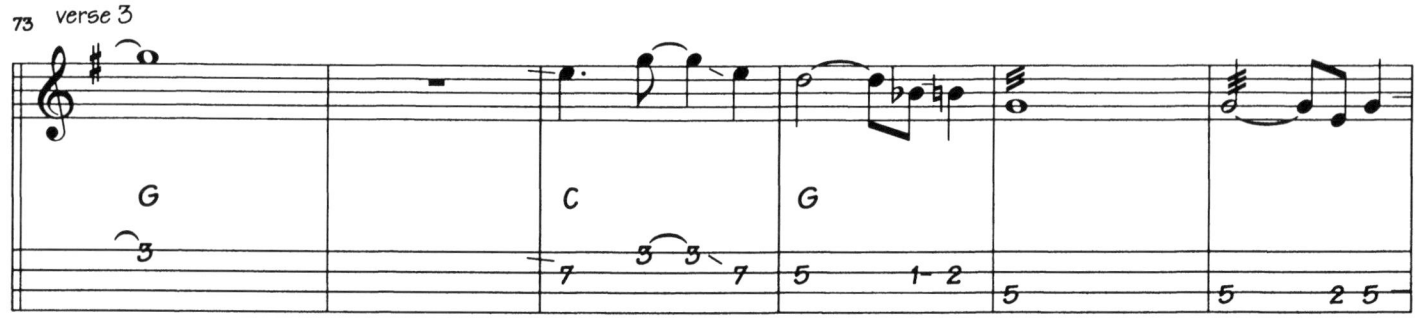

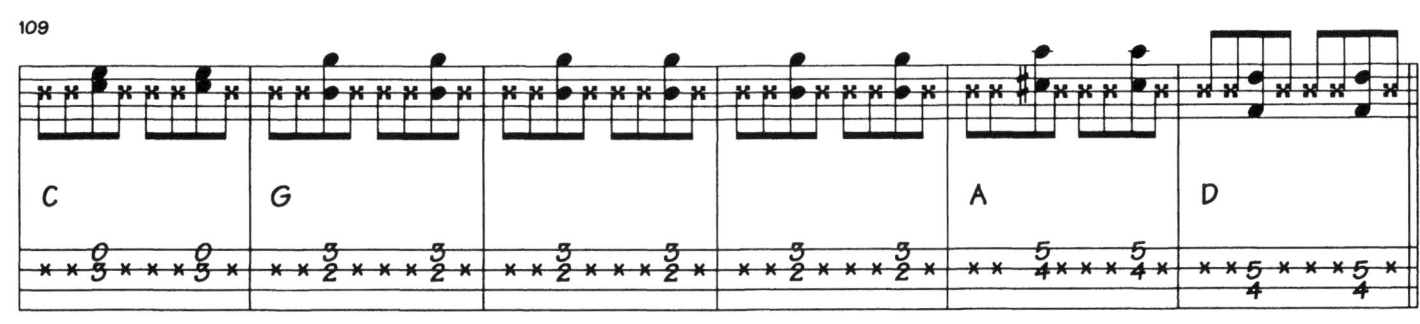

55

Dreadful Wind and Rain

This tune has a distinguishing 2/4 bar (bar 9). Old time tunes with this characteristic are sometimes referred to as "crooked tunes". There are countless examples of this type of tune, all of which sprout from a natural feel of phrasing rather than any intellectual attempt to be "different".

Dreadful Wind and Rain

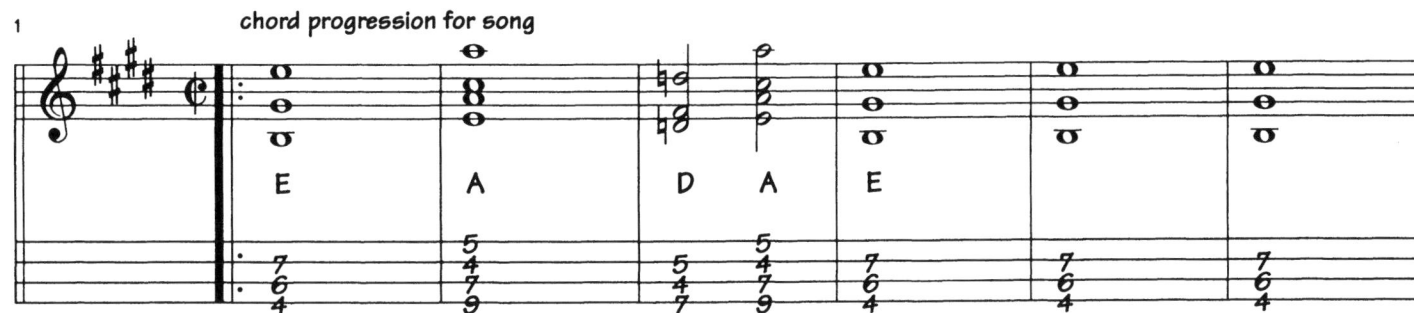
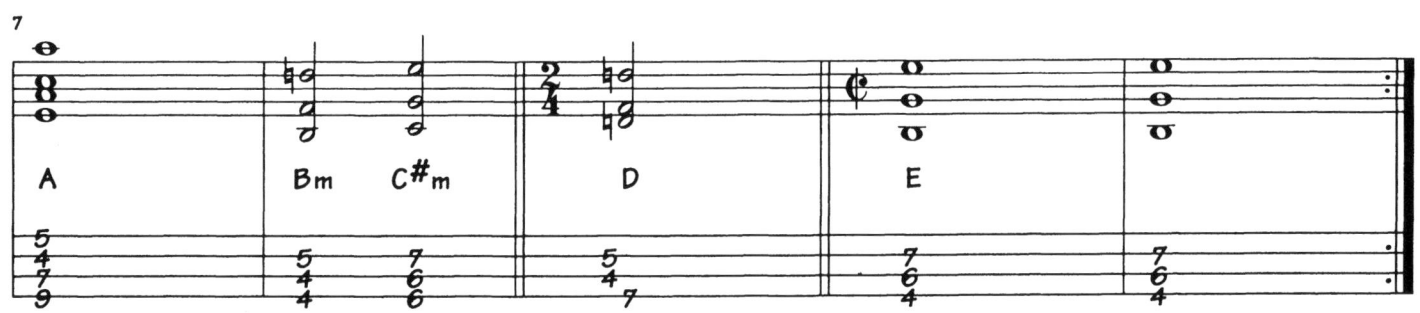

© Vegetiboy Music. All rights reserved. Used by permission.

*This page has been
left blank to avoid
awkward page turns*

The Handsome Cabin Boy

The intro is melody played with beautiful tremolo, and ends with two open string harmonics at the twelfth fret.

Solo 1 expands the melody with some tremolo applied to triplets in bars 86-87, 94-95. Note the open string harmonics again at the end of the passage.

Double stop tremolo begins at bar 124, breaking down into single note tremolo at 128.

The tremolo is left off the notes at 149 through 181, which breaks up the feeling nicely.

The ending solo brings the tune home with a single harmonic on the D string.

The Handsome Cabin Boy

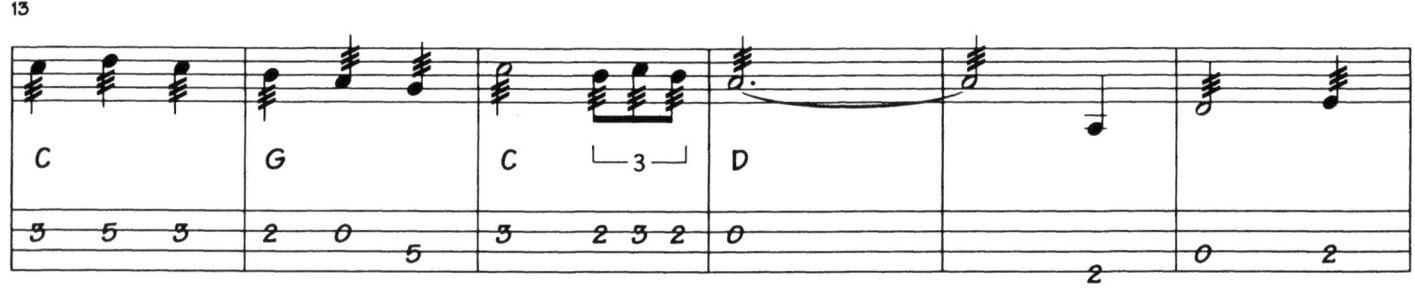

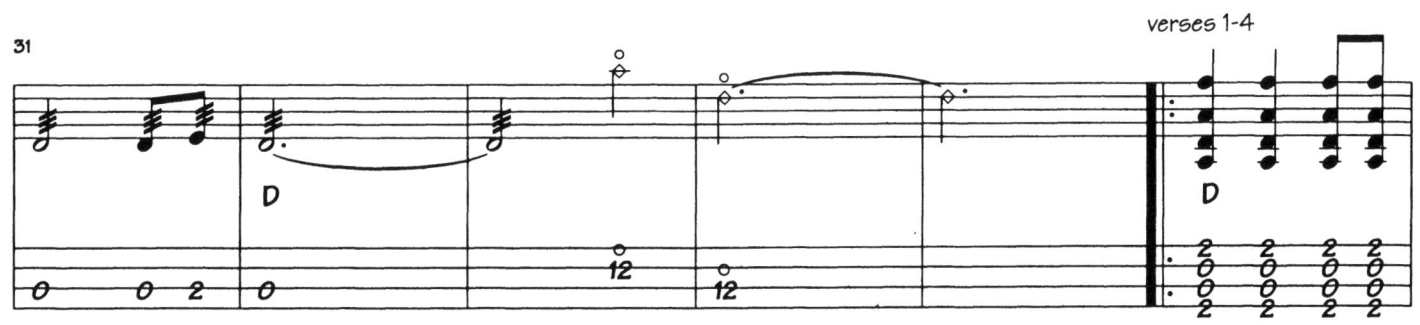
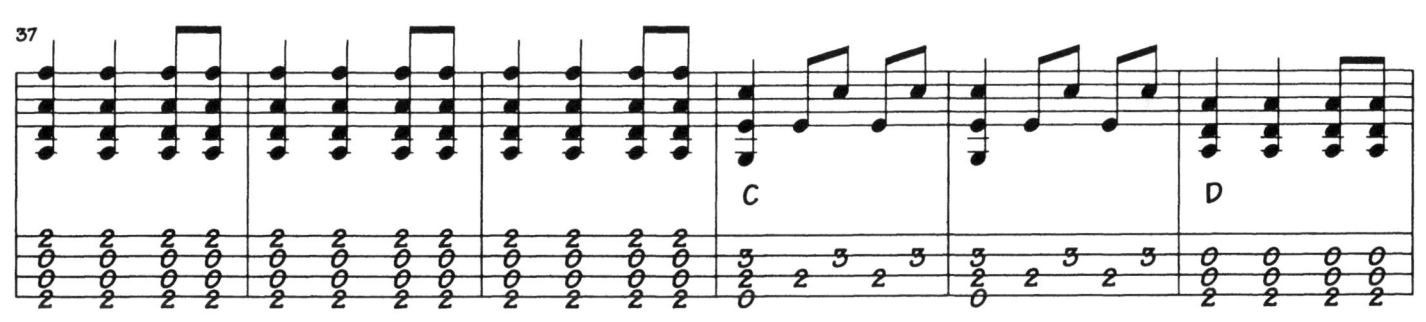

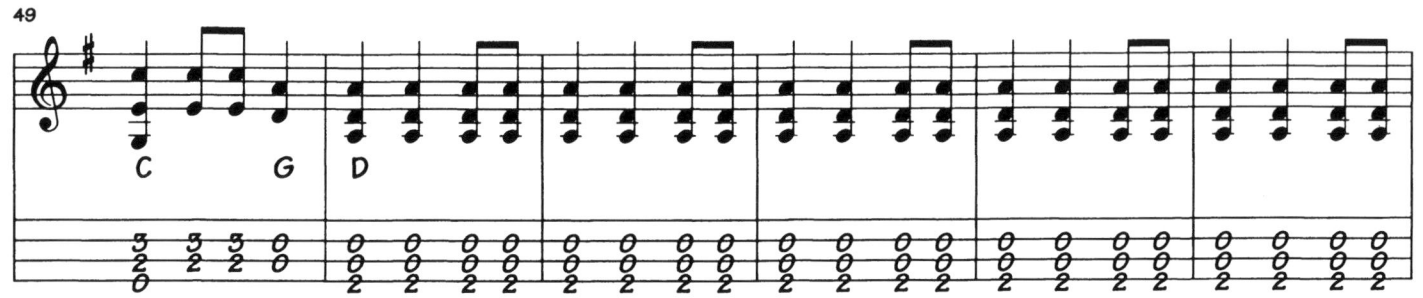

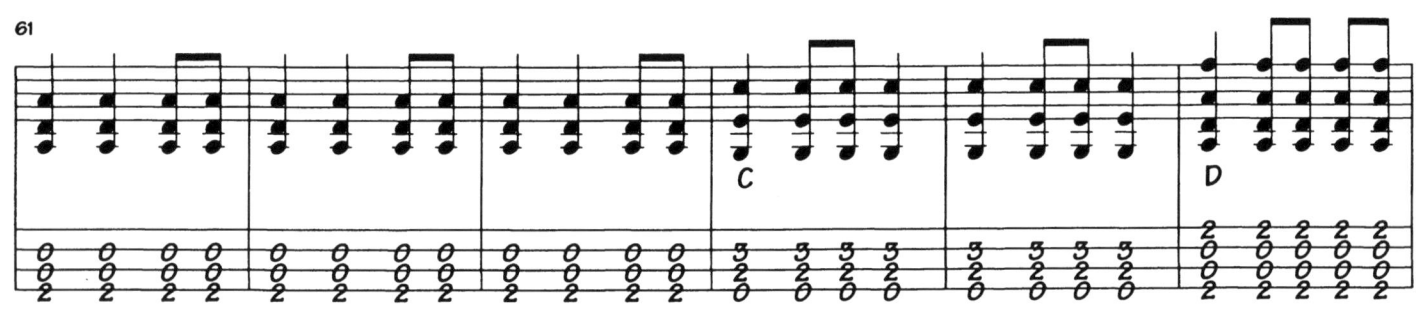
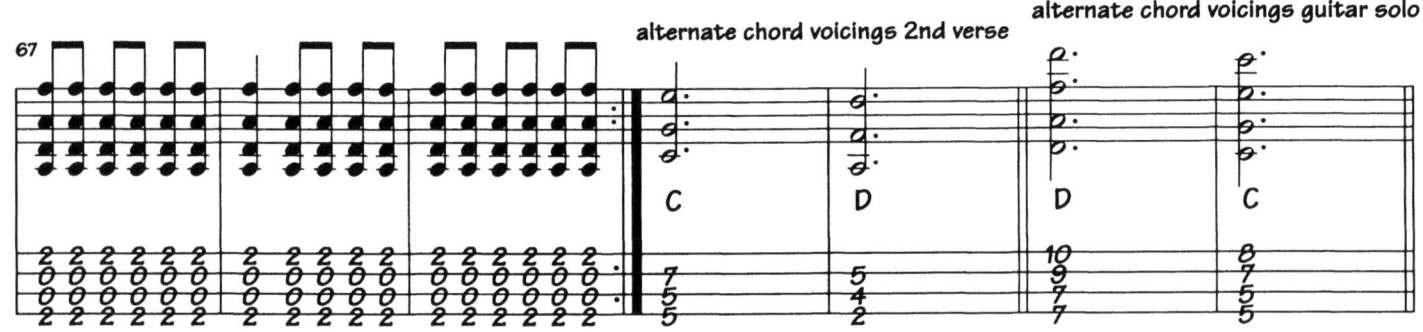

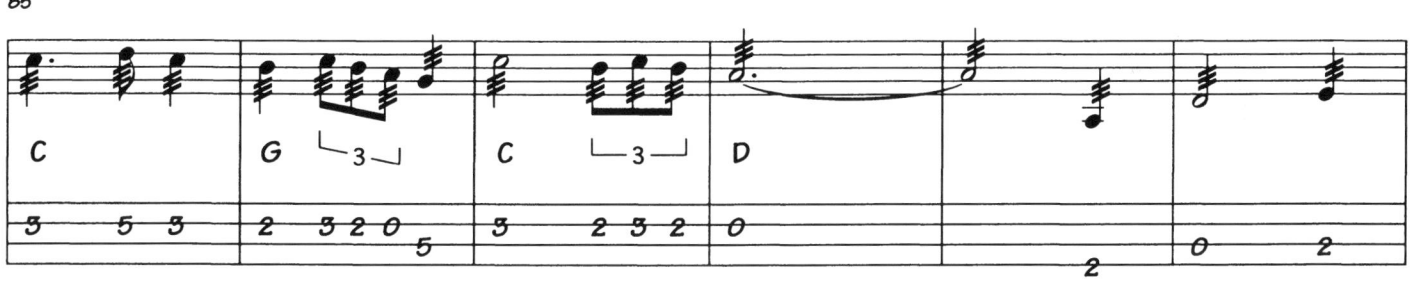

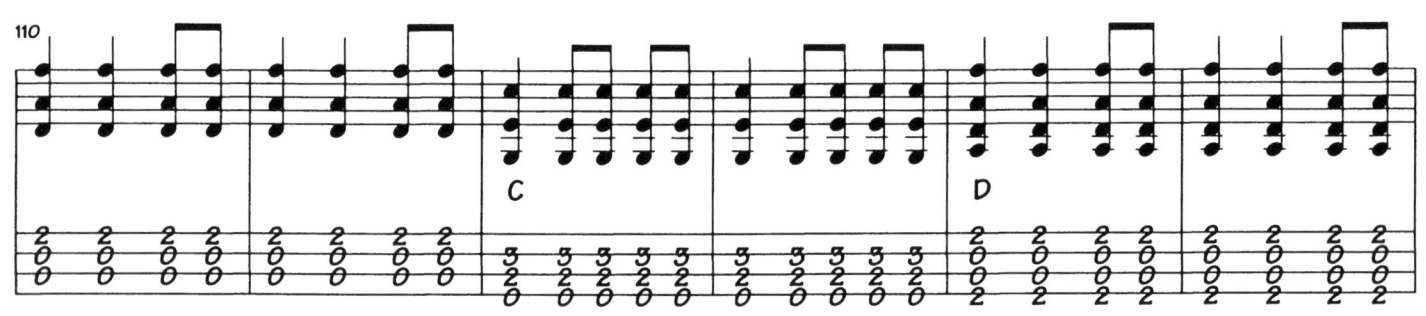
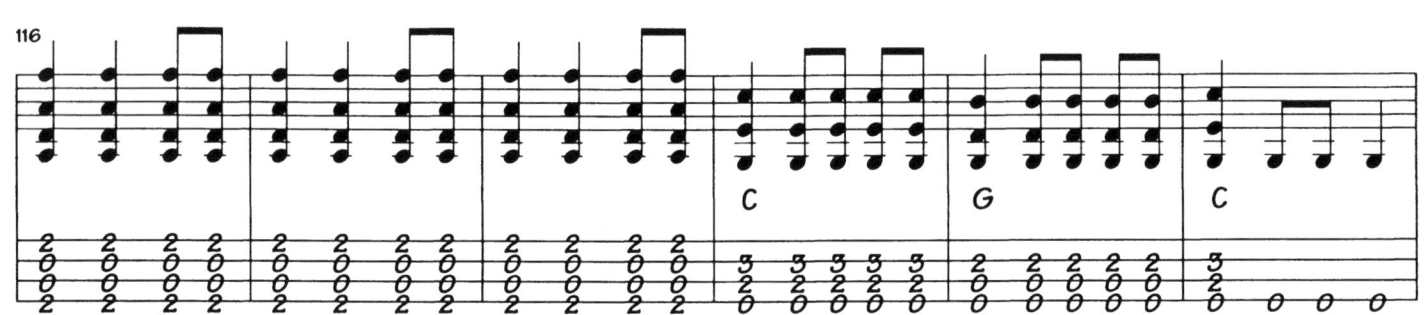

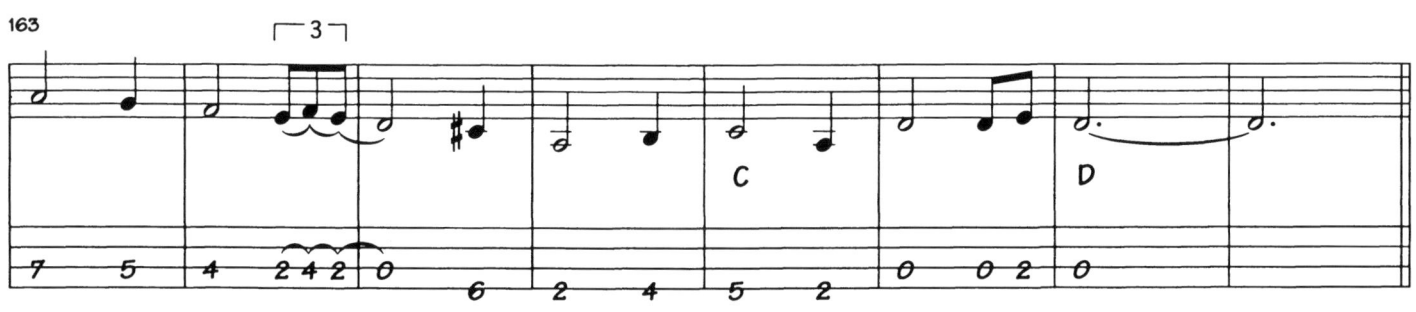

verse 6

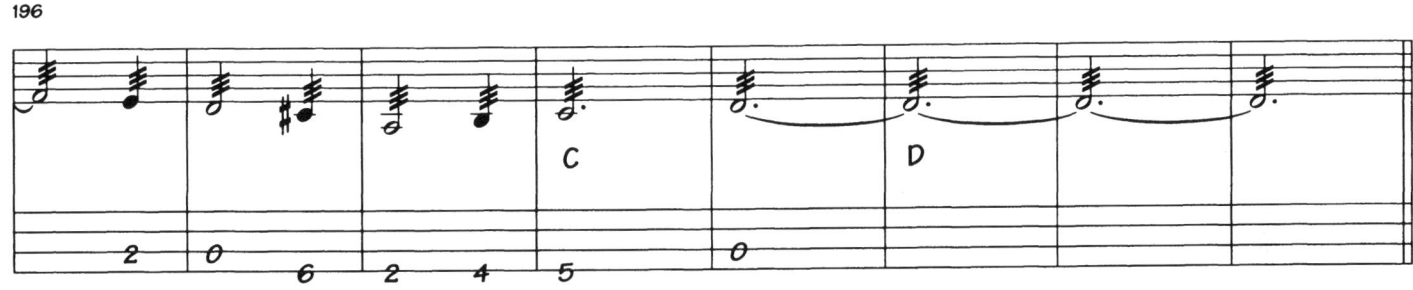

*This page has been
left blank to avoid
awkward page turns*

Whiskey in the Jar

This tune has become an Irish-American bar band staple. David's melody starts with a nice slide between the first three notes. Listen to the distinctive, warm tone of the third position, with the fingered E notes (2nd string, 7th fret) in contrast with the brighter sounding open E (1st string) in bar 20.

Note how the backup alternates between chord voicings, single note lines, and occasional long tones (chords that are held, rather than continually "chopped").

Bar 56 features an Fadd9 chord, an F triad with a G note on top. This is a departure from the usual triad (three note) chords used in traditional music, but the justification is that since the F chord and the G note are both part of the C scale (the home base of the song) and there is no dissonance between the notes, it works. Plus, it sounds great!

Chorus 4 (bar 111) is played with a chugging eighth note rhythm.

Solo 2 is strongly based on the melody and played in the higher octave.

The ending solo at bar 145 echoes the run up from low G (open 4th string) found in the chorus backup at bars 68 and 77.

Whiskey in the Jar

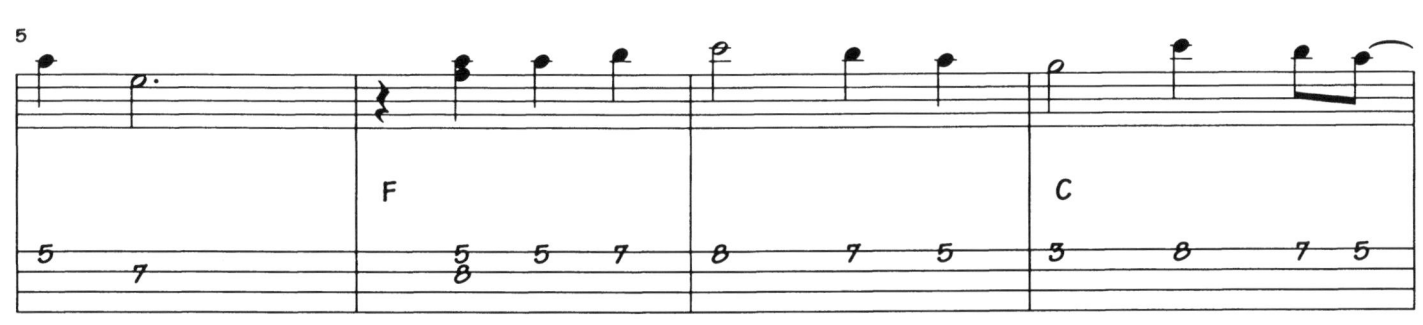
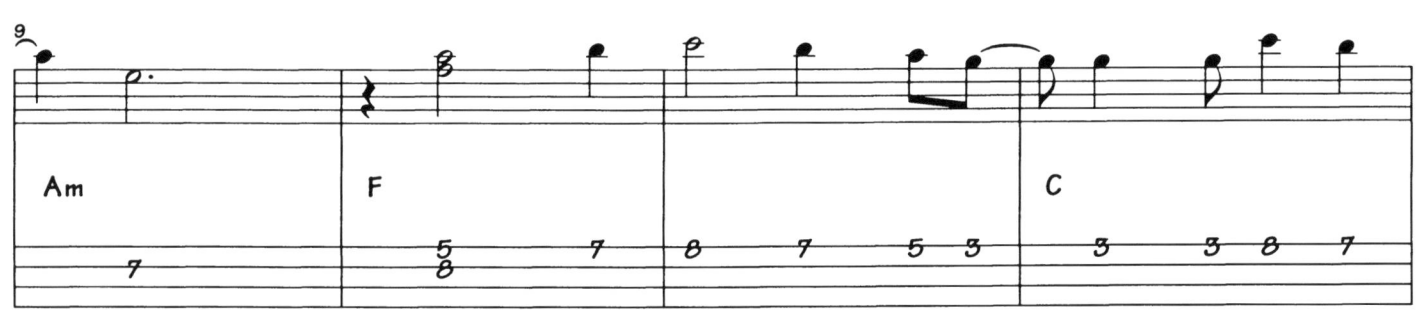

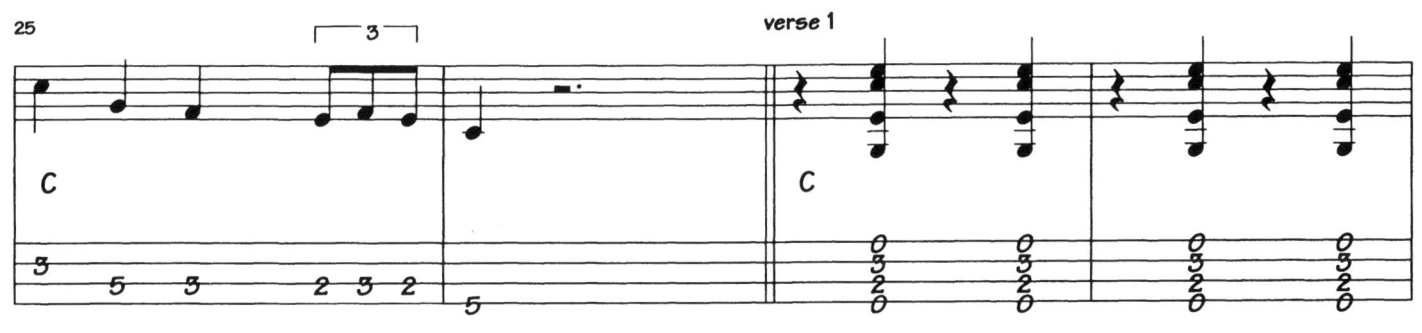

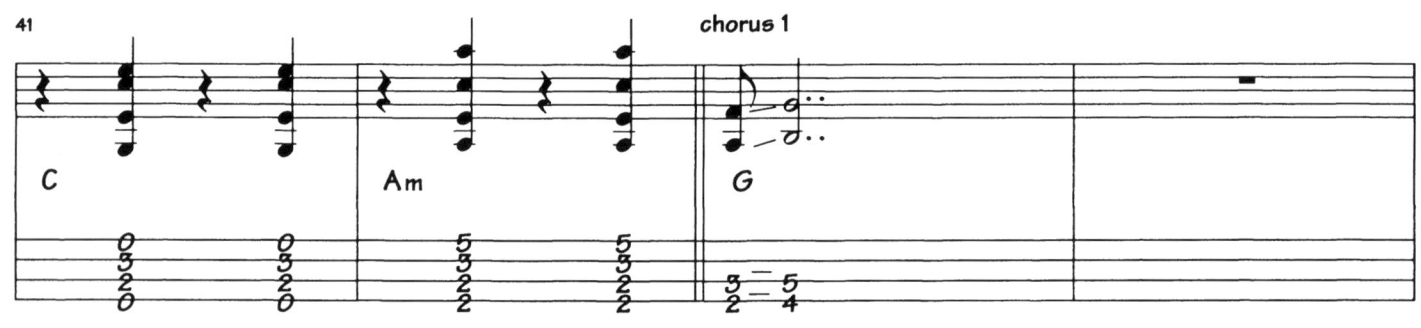
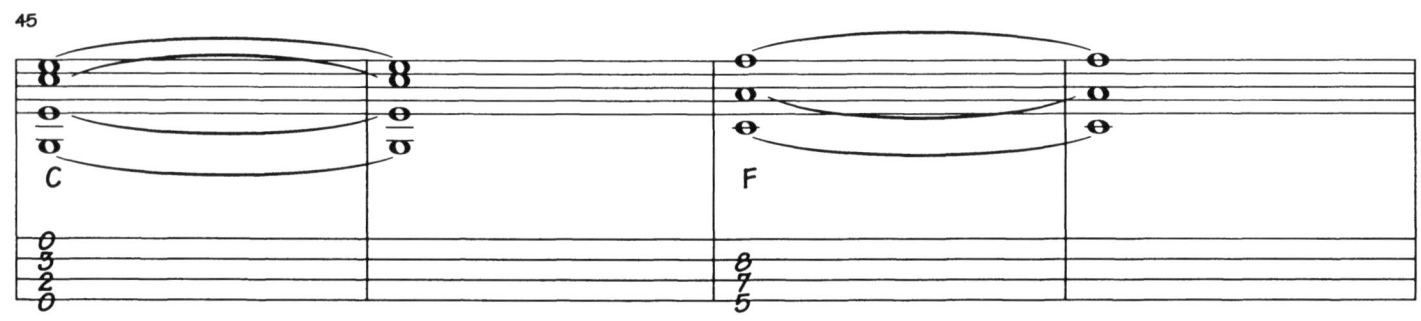

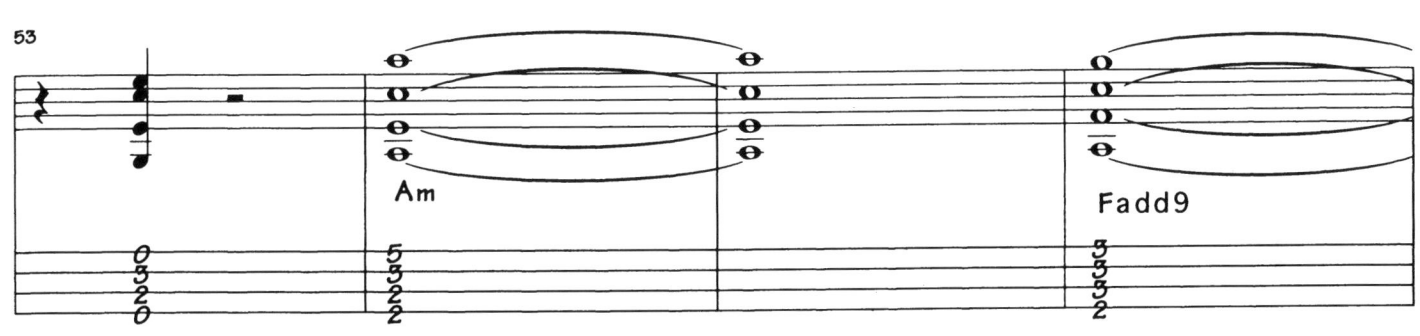
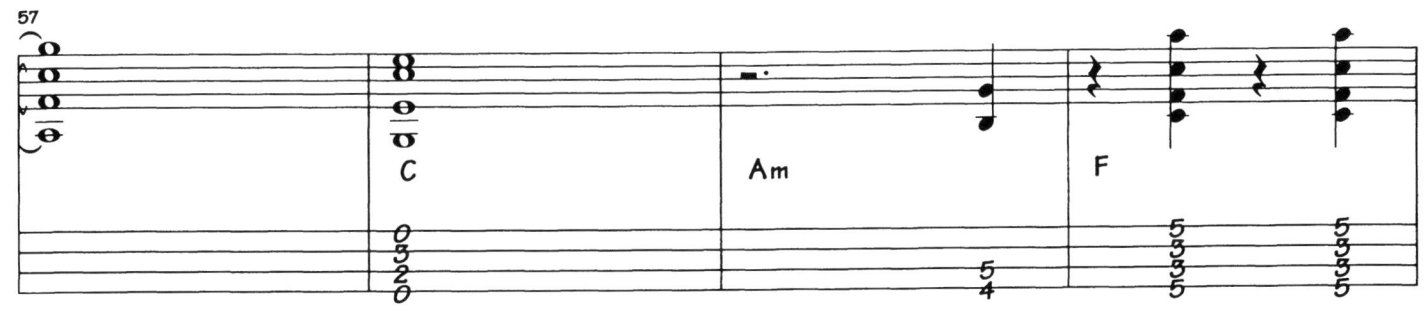

75

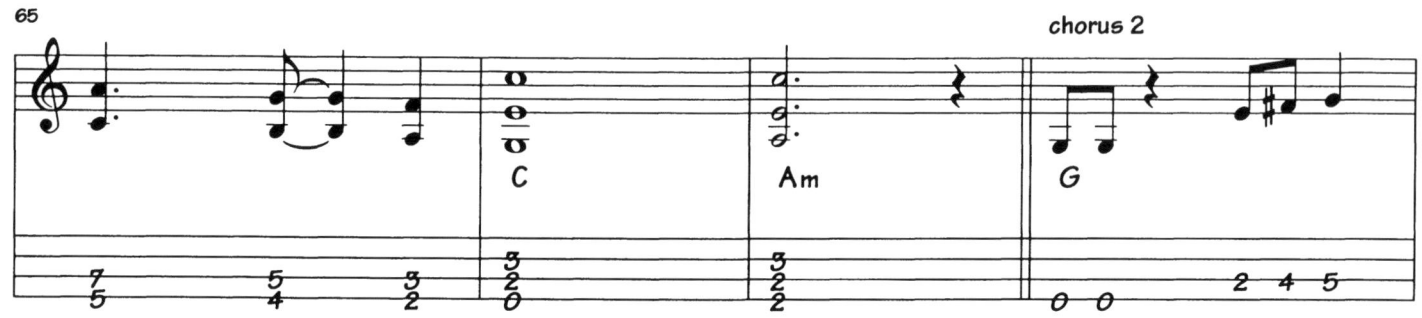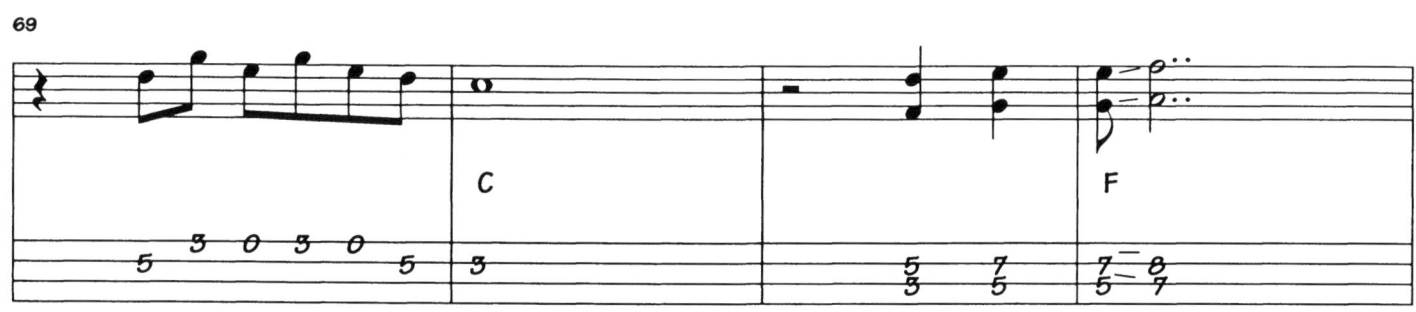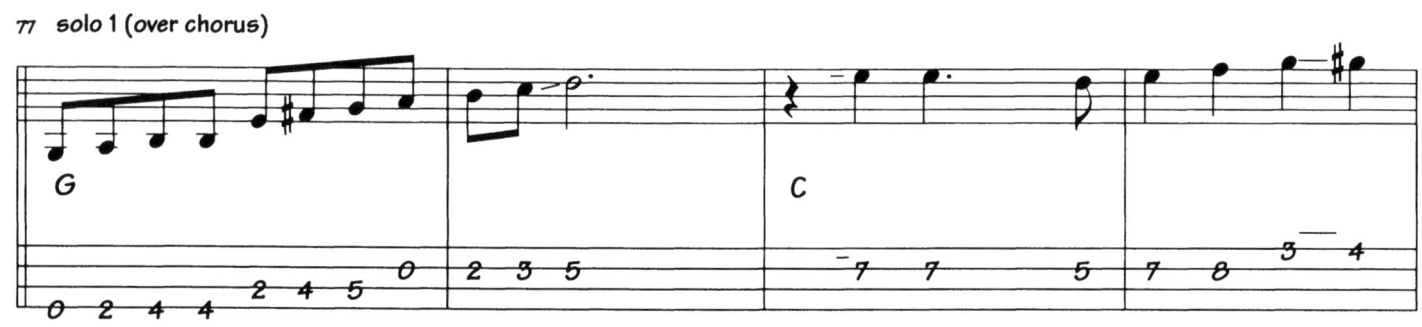

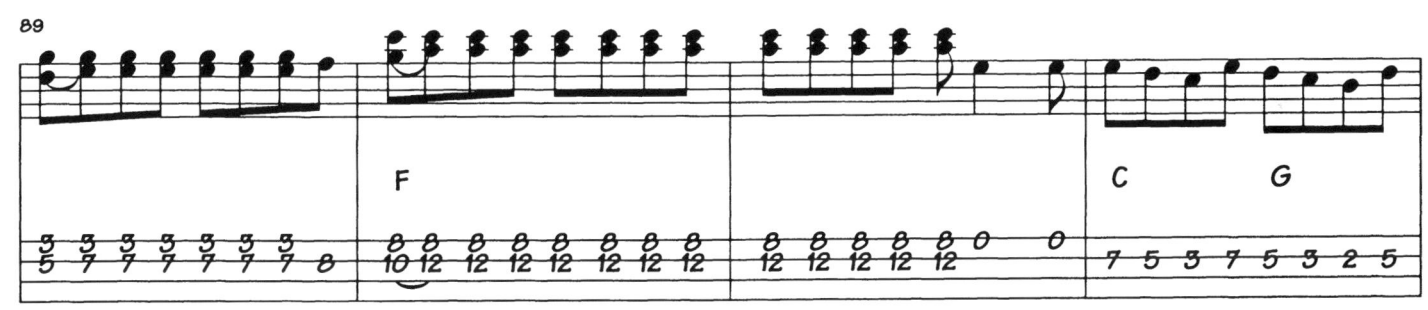

77

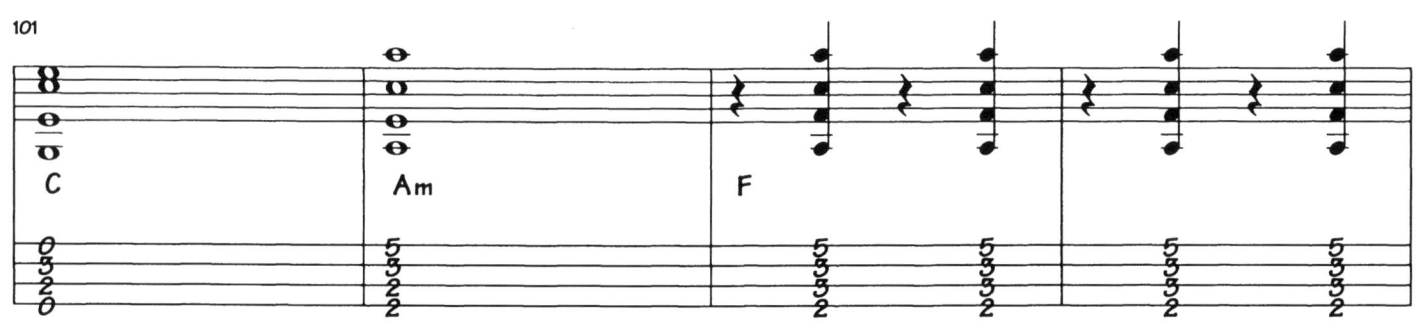
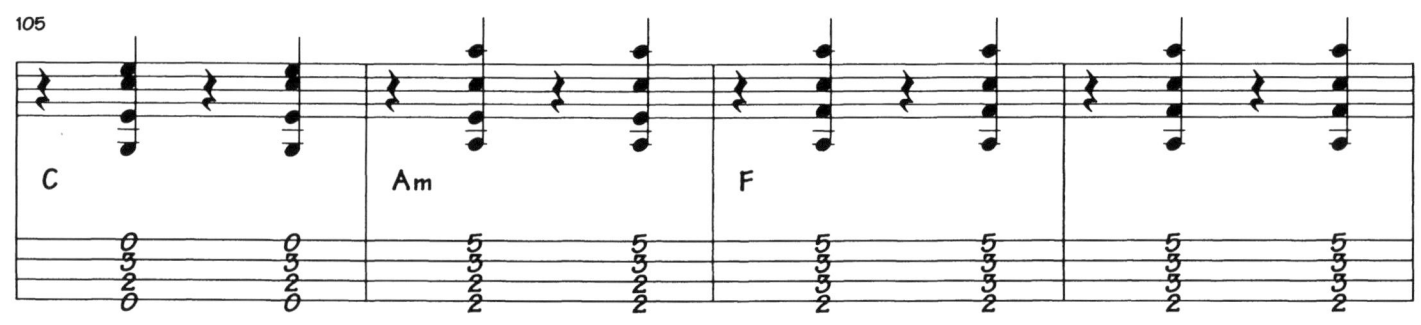
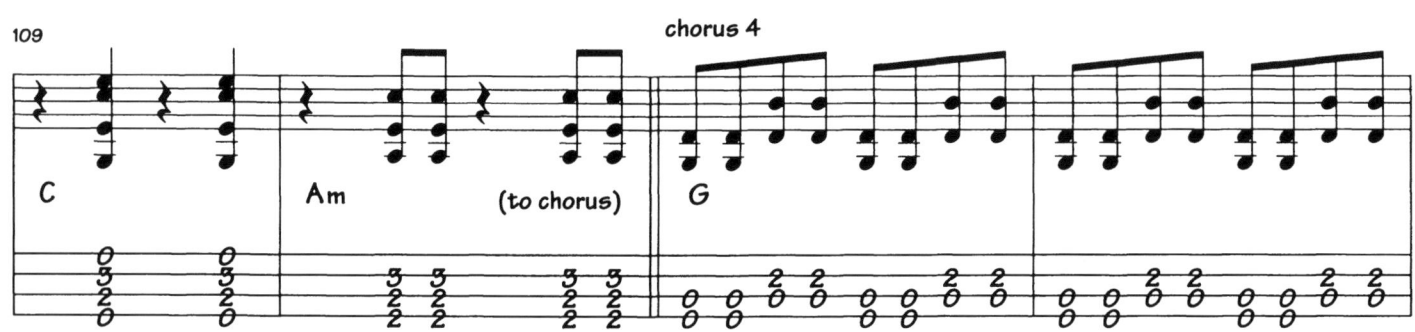

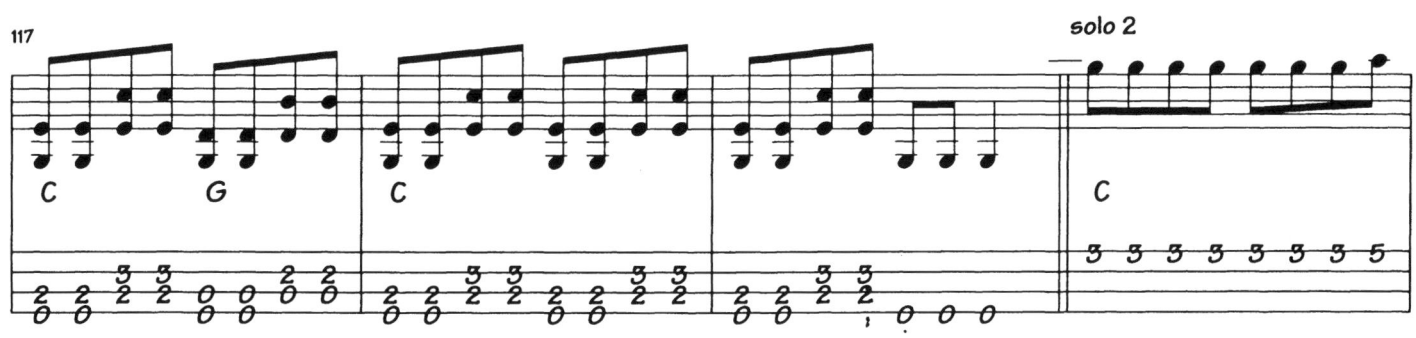
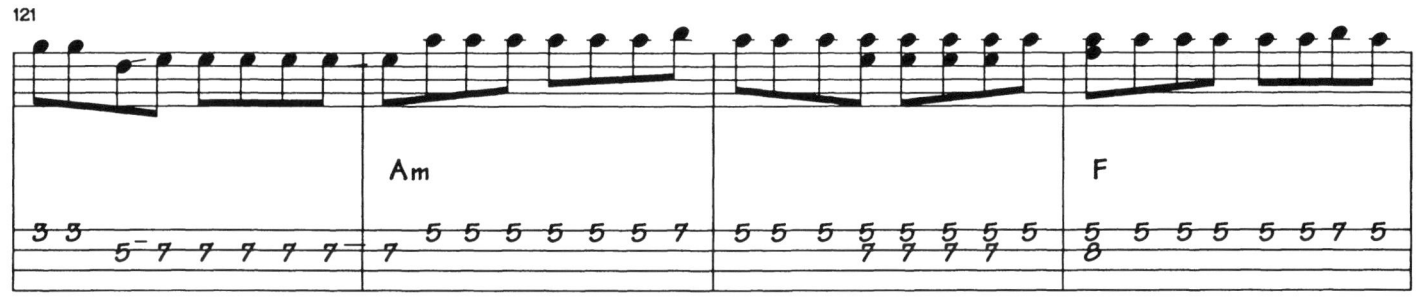

80

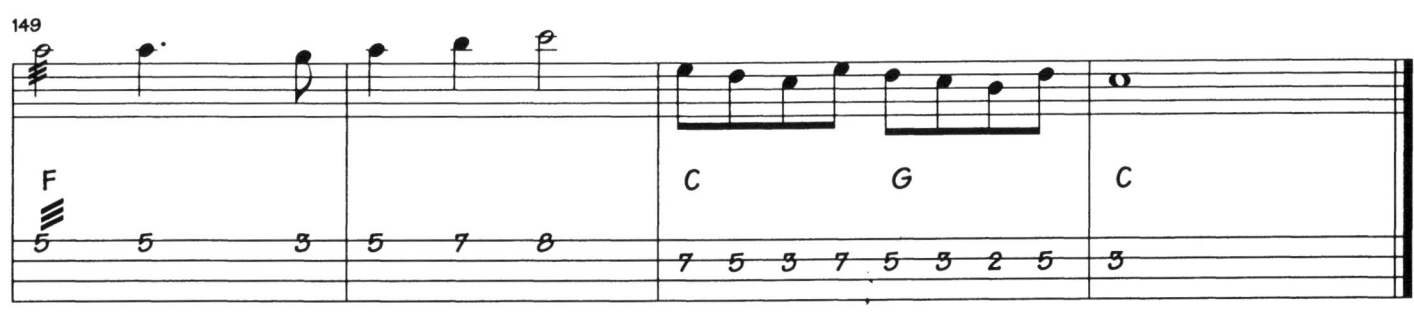

Down in the Valley

The album concludes with this lovely old Western standard.

Tremolo starts the first melody at bar 3, ending with a few chords at bars 14 and 15. The backup under the verse goes into a triplet rhythm alternating on two notes at bar 19, which can be seen as a kind of slow tremolo.

Solo 1 at 45 starts with a line walking up on the last two notes of a triplet. The solo alternates between tremolo and non tremolo notes.

Verse 2 gets back to the triplets at bar 63, and chords at bar 74. The bar of rest at 87 sets up a long note at 88 and a return to tremolo at bar 90. At bars 92-93, listen how the F♯ on string 3 is sustained with tremolo while the B♭ and A are added on string 4.

The harmonica solo at bar 116 gets simple chordal accompaniment up to bar 129, which gets a melodic interjection.

Verse 4 has some Monroe style blues phrases at bar 147.

The last solo is a harmony to Jerry's melody, and ends the album with elegant simplicity.

Down in the Valley

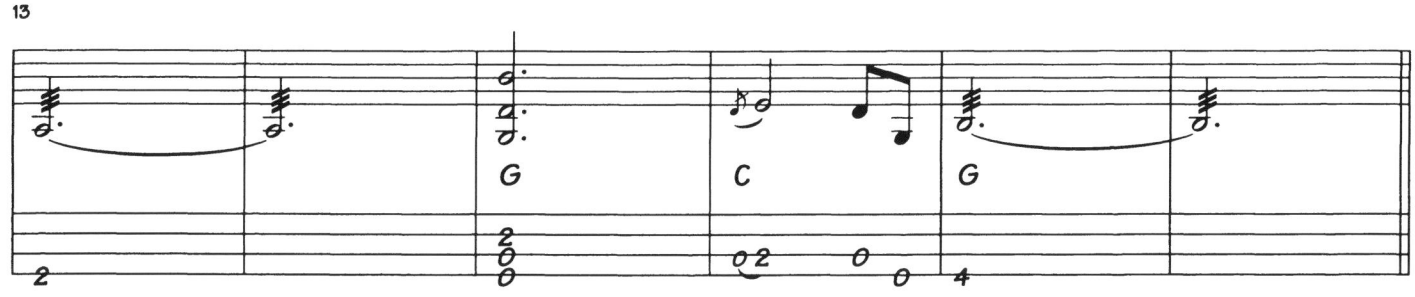

© DAWG Music. All rights reserved. Used by permission.

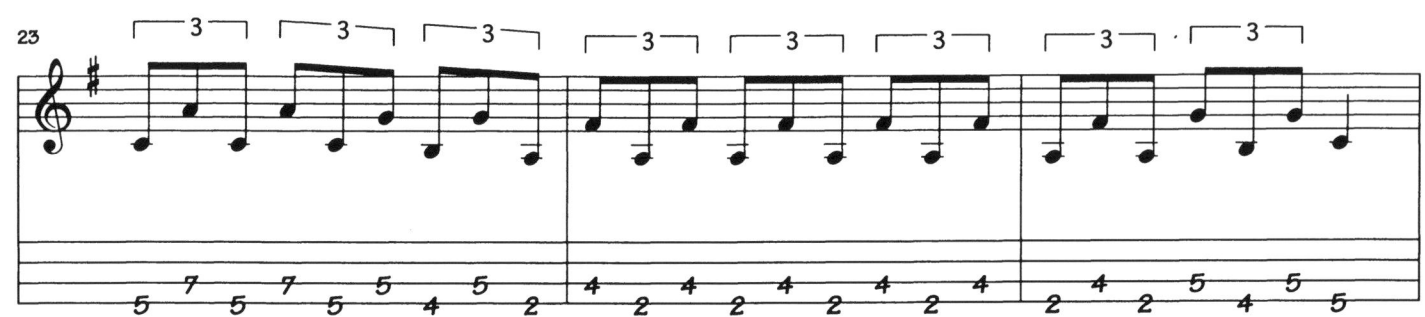

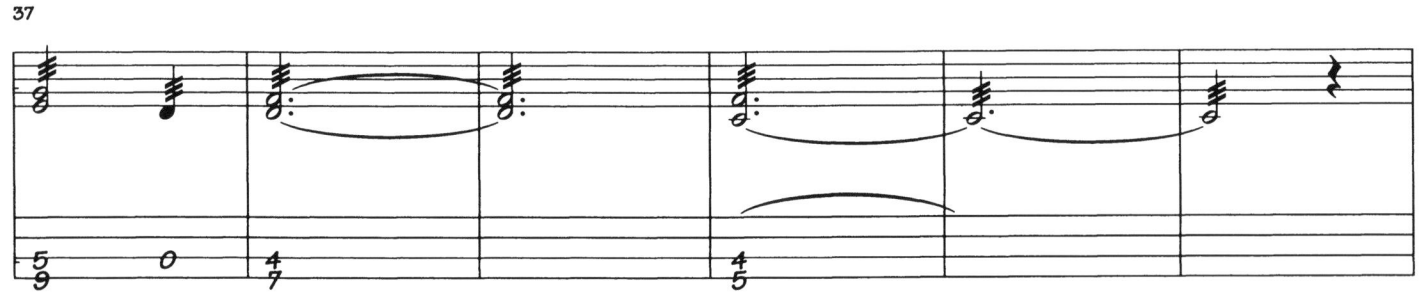

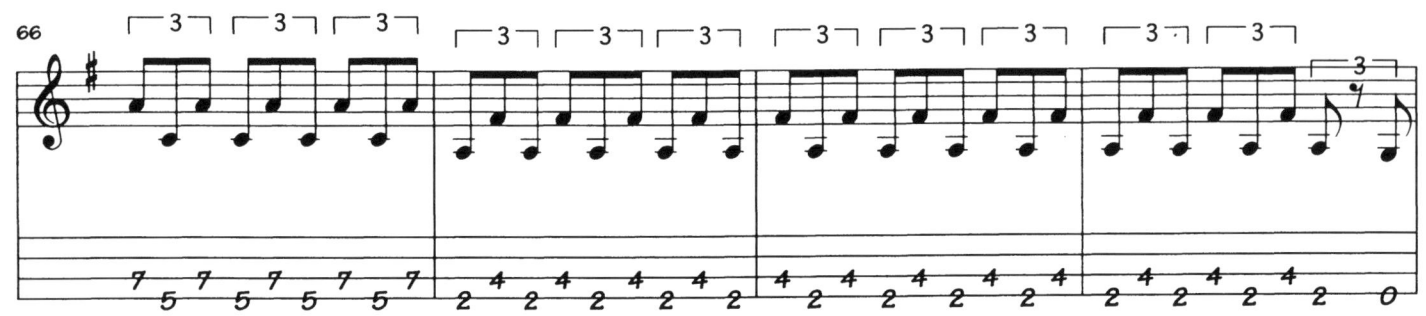

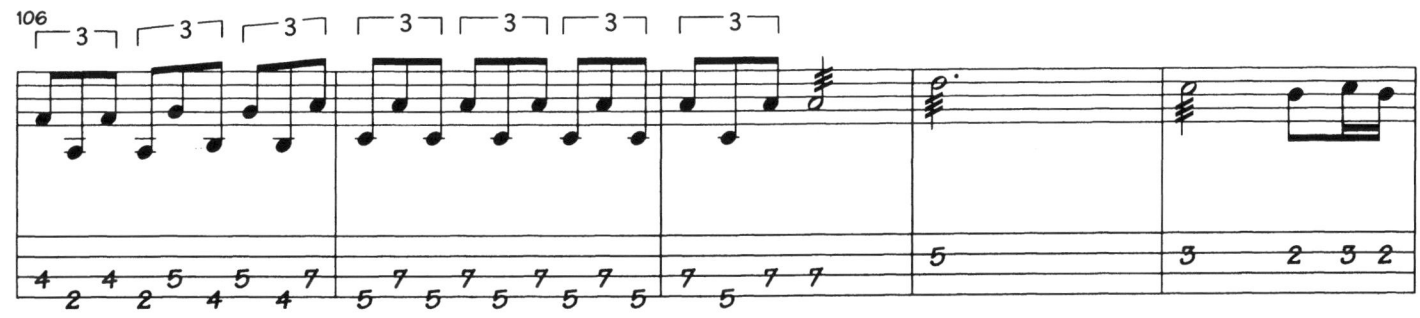

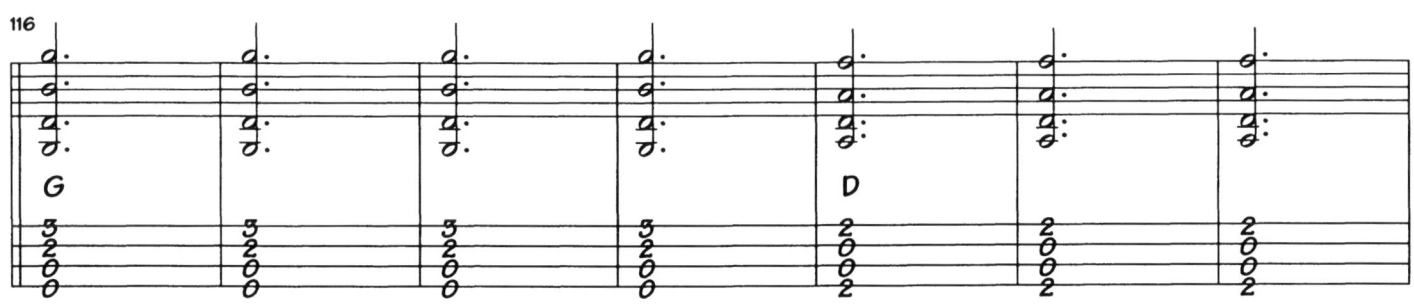

Harmonica solo

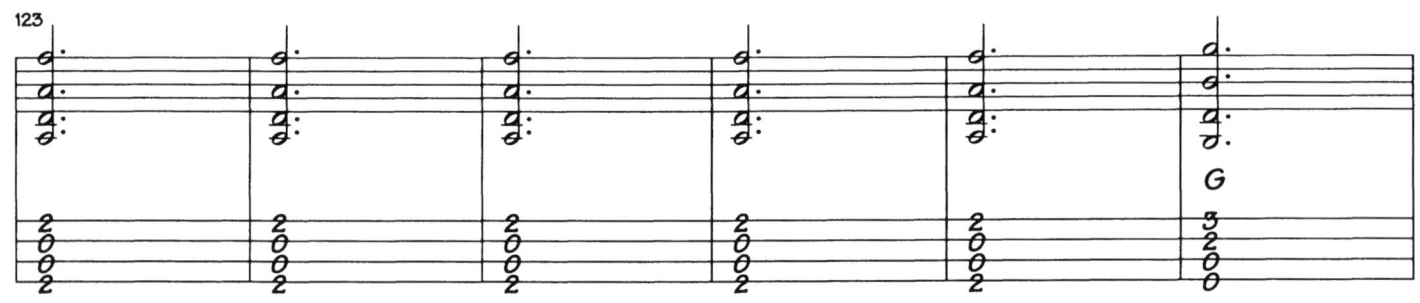

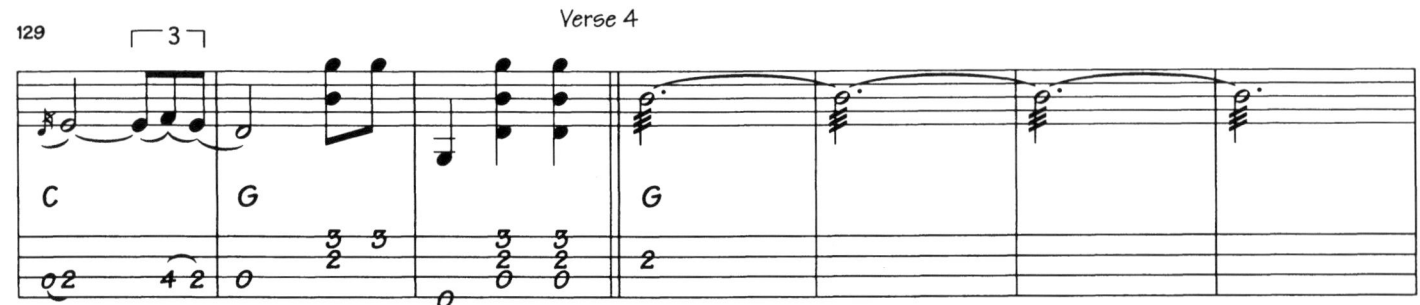

Verse 4

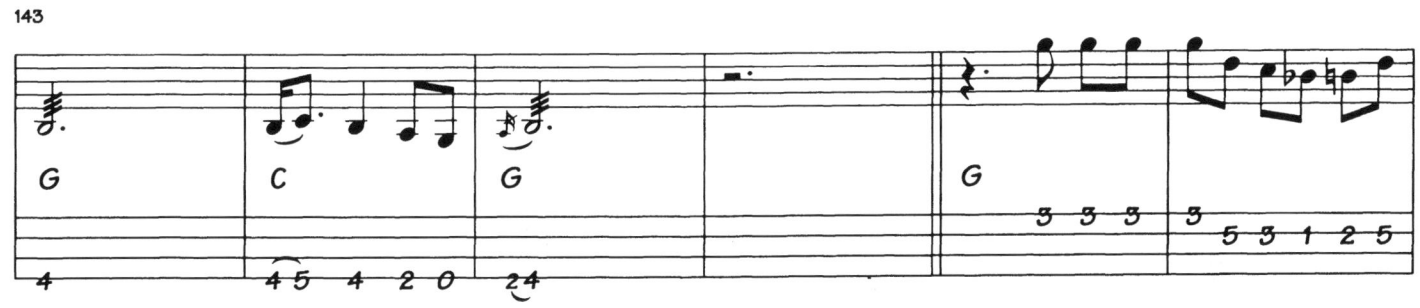

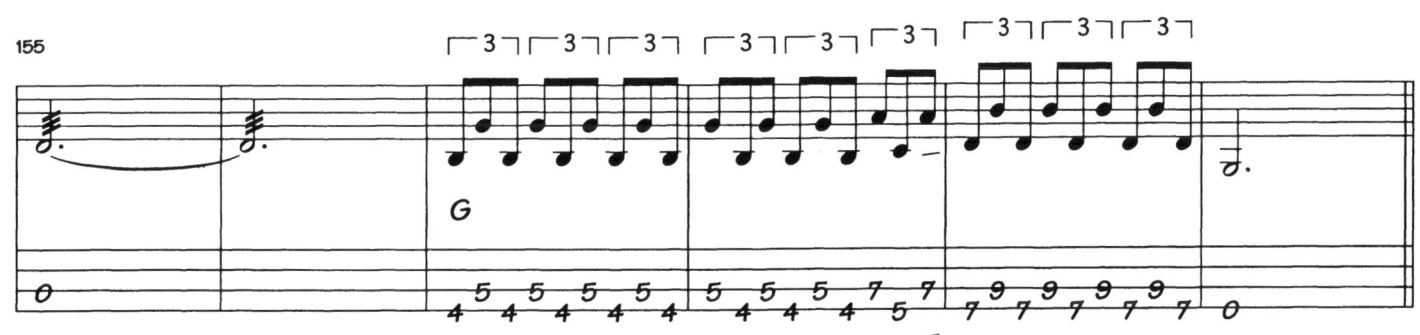

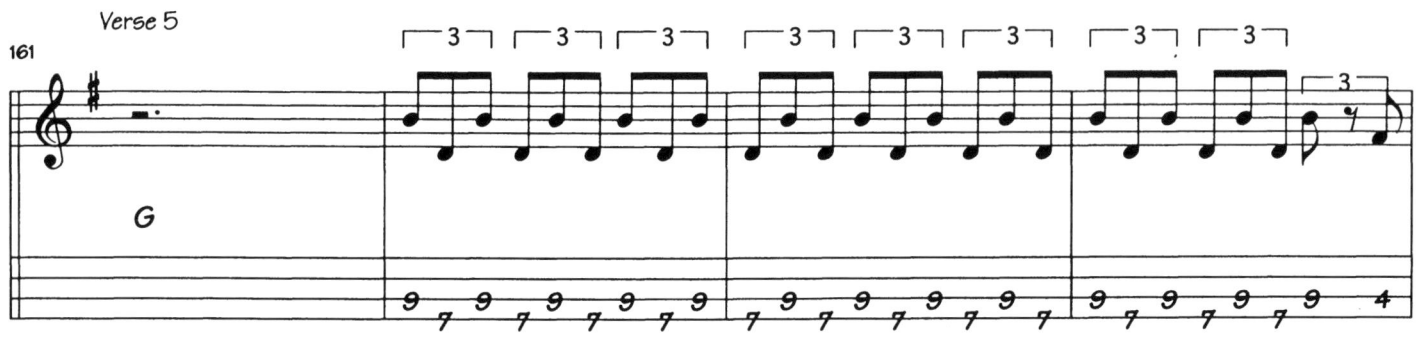
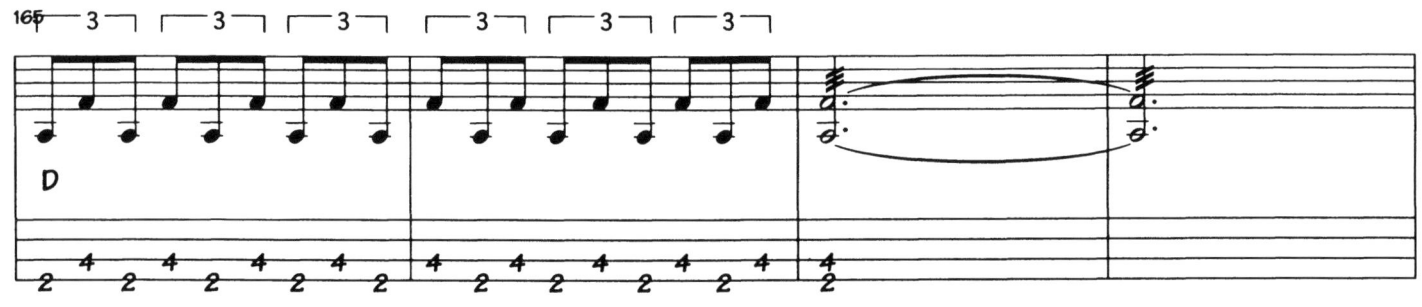
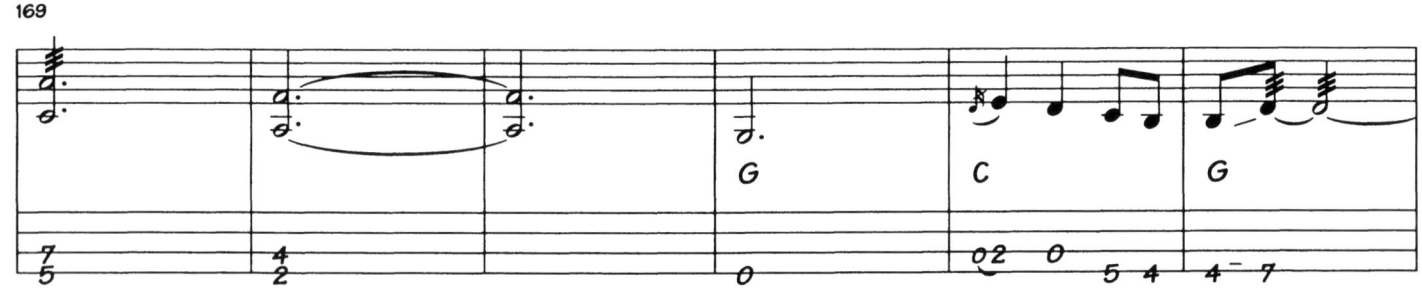
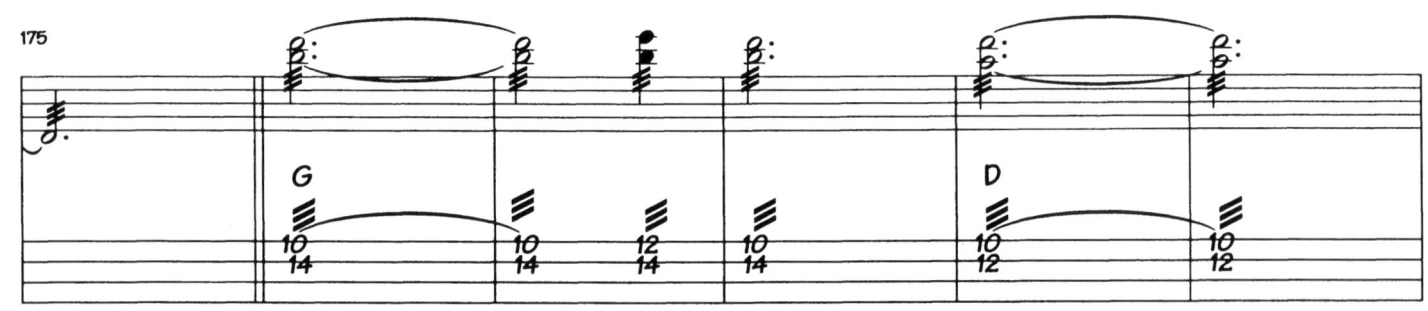

Transcriber's Bio

John McGann is a Boston based mandolinist and guitarist, composer, arranger, teacher and transcriber; member of The Wayfaring Strangers (with Matt Glaser, Tony Trischka, Andy Statman etc.) and Rust Farm (with Chris Moore, Richard Gates and Dave Mattacks). He won 1st Place at the National Mandolin Championship, Winfield Kansas (1985). John writes for *Flatpicking Guitar Magazine, Mandolin Magazine, Acoustic Guitar Magazine* as well as Mel Bay publications, including an upcoming book on the octave mandolin. He is the staff transcriber for David Grisman's Acoustic Disc website (www.acousticdisc.com). For more info, please visit www.johnmcgann.com